Ramadan CONSCIENCE

About the author

Born in Canada in 1947 as Norman Paul Sutherland, he arrived in the UK 1973 becoming a British citizen in 1985. In the 1990s, at university, he gained his writer's name, Paul Sutherland. 2004 he became a Sufi Muslim adopting Paul Abdul Wadud Sutherland. Since then he has had 19 poetry collections published and has edited a range of other titles. He founded the literary arts journal *Dream Catcher* in 1995-96. His *New and Selected Poems* came out from Valley Press in 2017: 384 pages of 45 years of writings. *Ramadan Conscience* is his second book by Beacon Books, the first: *The Servant of Loving One*. He lives with his wife in Lincolnshire. www.authorpaulsutherland.com

Previously Published Poems

'A Poor Man's Ramadan': an earlier version was first published in *Poems on the Life of Prophet Muhammad*, Muslim Academic Trust, 2014

'The Fast' first published in *Poems on the Life of Prophet Muhammad*, Muslim Academic Trust, 2014

'Thunderstorm Afternoon During Ramadan' first published in the *Pop Up Anthology*, edited by Janice Windle, 2013

'The Mosque Party' first published in *Child Roots*, Partnerships Publishing, 2024

'The Pen' first published in *Only Words*, Vellum Publishing, 2023

'Last Minute Rush' first published in *Kaleidoscope of Stories (Muslim Voices in Contemporary Poetry)*, Lote Tree Press, 2020

Ramadan CONSCIENCE

Paul Abdul Wadud Sutherland

BB

BEACON BOOKS

Published in the UK by Beacon Books and Media Ltd
Earl Business Centre, Dowry Street, Oldham, OL8 2PF, UK.

www.beaconbooks.net

ISBN: 978-1-915025-21-0 Paperback
ISBN: 978-1-915025-22-7 Hardback
ISBN: 978-1-915025-23-4 eBook

Cataloging-in-Publication record for this book is available from the British Library

Cover design by Raees Mahmood Khan

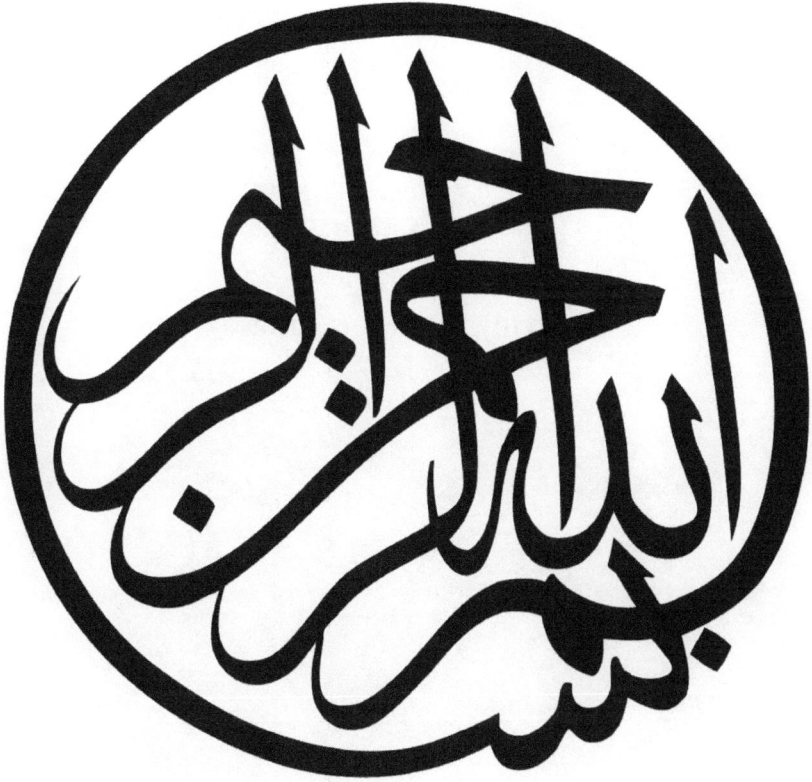

Dedication

To my wife Hajja Afifa

Contents

A Poor Man in Ramadan   1
Ramadans Across the Season   2
Iftar in a Car Park   7
Enroute and Arrival: the east coast   10
The Artist   12
Thunder Afternoon during Ramadan   16
Ramadan Moments   18
First Day of Ramadan   38
A Ramadan Night   42
Ramadan Journal   43
The Mosque Party   50
From Three Dreams   51
My Mum Passed in Ramadan 1438 in Canada   66
To my Mum Ramadan, Canada   69
In Home's Summer Garden   74
Twentieth Nocturne   77
Three *fajrs* in Central London, UK   78
Ramadan Quatrains written during *itiqaf*   *80*
In Egypt   94
Notes from the Belovéd   97
Another Day's Fascinations   99
In Alexandria   101
Final Day Light   110
Mysteries of Faith   112
Seclusion at Home   114
Precession   117
The Fast   118
On The Verge of Fasting   120
Peterborough Lyrics   121
The Pen   132
Miniatures from Recent Fasts   133
Last Minute Rush   136
Eve of Eid   137
IT   138

A Poor Man in Ramadan

I was a young man who not long before
had pledged to be a Muslim, keeping the faith,
believing in One God and honouring His Messenger.

And yet I abused my fast, having sex with my wife,
during the forbidden day hours after cock-crow.
My conscience demanded that I should go

to Muhammad, peace be upon him. I hurried alone
to where he sat with his companions among palm-shadow
(no one stopped me). I told him of my offence and my regret.

He didn't react as if I'd performed a fatal error but said *go
and provide a meal for a Muslim in poverty, or someone
in hardship and through this giving find forgiveness.*

I answered I had no resources to buy food. The Blessed,
the Utterly Fair, looked at me searching. *Then give some dates
to a person.* I can't afford dates, my response, even for my family.

A load of the dark fruit, heaped in baskets, arrived on camel-back.
But none moved to eat one, though I could see their succulence.
The appetite of his followers had been subdued by the fast.

Muhammad, considering my case, paused to reflect. At last
exclaimed, *have some of this harvest, here* - loading my hands
with ripe dates – *and go and feed your wife and children.* I carried

them home through grass-kerbed roads, by castle walls of the rich.
From the Generous of Allah, my two cupped hands turned more
and more sticky. I half stumbled across abundant blue iris.

Ramadans Across the Season

Dedicated to Afifa Emutallah

Ramadan Sequence
Late Summer

Pure lilies caress
on our Ramadan table
zinc-white cyclamen

hacking for *Iftar*
to dive into a fresh bag
of hot Bombay Mix

for Afifa

gazing blue-skyward
through buddleia – passing clouds
turn to butterflies

this year, the swifts left
early to circle God's House
during Ramadan

like us all fasting
sunflowers in Allah's wind
bow and bow and bow

her head to *qibla*
we might yet bed-in tansies
by a love one's grave

visiting neighbours
in Islam – we find their home
on the second try

before breaking fast
we chant many *salawat*,
to Muhammad – peace

lengthening hushed voice –
rose hips on the cloudy cloth
following *taraweh*

a joyful clutter
after evening and darkness
steel pots crowd the sink

nite-lites long smothered:
saving a mid-morning moth –
your hands' tender cage

stuck on the door frame
a rigid daddy-long-legs'
frail calligraphy

in a mild temper
our neighbour trims back ivy
snipping her clothesline

steaming cauliflowers
drift up to the garden wall
and winter wood pile

succeeding *zuhr*
hours sow an expectancy
harvested at sun-set

somebody's covered
lush plums in an oval dish
to protect their eyes

from a tower's cap
a mourning dove *voos* and *voos*...
all demons in irons

Allah's ladybird
on the broken bench's arm ...
propped hijabs riffle

in bloom once again
masquerade's pink, yellow-rouge
by the bruised back door

each of us naked
before the Lord – His mercies
out racing our fear

His gaze caressing
as if our skin didn't exist,
the heart's shell shattered

in fallen pear shape
isha's moon shades to primrose
a splitting cloudbank

cheeping sparrows queue
on the arch – waiting their turn
with the shy feeder

on the blue table
perfumed cyclamen shelter
rain-speckled lilies

afternoon sun burst,
printing the wall, slants across
the *ka'ba*'s ley-line

our Thursday's fast ends,
a big blackberry crumble ...
each one's hands soon red

For Muhammad (saws)

he sliced his turban's
blessed cloth to make a hijab
for a scared slave girl

dates and new mint tea
then we angle prayer rugs
for twilight's *maghrib*

white stones – for counting
taraweh's twenty *rakats* –
clack on the hearth beam

rescued from pain's grasp
the moon enters the white nights
above collapsed roofs

grown weak past midnight
into God's suffering Truth
we plunge with His Book

Turkish coffee's sting
to keep our vigil – who knows
angels could descend

street curtains eased back
to conserve electricity.
In dawn's night, we pray.

Iftar in a Car Park

Engine off, at twilight, I open the glove compartment to retrieve sandwiches dedicated for break-of- fast. This incident marked the earliest Ramadans for the new revert. I had often observed the pinks and heliotropes of the afterglow; now they possessed an ethical value. The diurnal change carried the significance that the end of day unlocked the potential for nourishment after sunlight's fade. It was mid-autumn, the evening wandered ahead in my thoughts towards a recital I was being paid to perform at a local poetry appreciation group. I rested in a unfamiliar setting, finding a discreet place to park; pray and break the day's abstaining, near St Albans. I remember the inner and outer topography. My nervousness about the event ahead but also being a fresh Sufi Muslim with a strong Christian background. I could be distracted by the historgraphy of the sainted Roman who was one of the first to bring Christianity to Britain. Heavy tree-shadows hung over the car; between the canopies the colourful traces of the day could be discerned with implication that expanding night demanded obedience to my new articles of faith that enforced the fast and its hesitant release. I knew going without food and drink represented the essence of many beliefs but that ancient Christ-carrier worried in the back of my mind. He was born long before Muhammad, Allah's blessing and peace be upon him. I debated whether to switch the engine on to circulate warmth or not; the simple refreshments were tasty. I tried to catch each crumb before it fell on my 'poetic' clothing. My new faith, Islam, was somehow squeezed between that timeless Christian martyr, St Alban, far ahead of Christendom, and my desire to write and perform poetry. Yet against the evidence of my traditional preoccupations it was clear that something else breathed, compelling this unanticipated stop on the way to a chosen planned event. None in that small future room with pre-formed chairs with its aire of modernity would want to hear about this preliminary pause. Their friendly and sometimes less friendly faces won't hear mystic chanting in my poems that made my wife declare 'you have always been a Sufi, a real believer'. My marriage to her by degrees had led to submitting to the needs and practice of Ramadan. Being a novice Muslim, Islam seemed alien but I forecast it would grow to overwhelm old promises. Perhaps, my transformation was similar to how Jesus at the last supper highlighted the lesser ingredients on the table, the bread and wine, supplanting the Jewish passover lamb. Now the communion host was being overwhelmed by remembrance of the One God, Allah, without partners, and no style of nutriment could represent or encapsulate that remembrance or *zikr*. Instead, observance of daylight's wan and at these longitudes, with the subtle emergence of nightfall (that didn't end but began a new day) hinted at a changed manner of thinking and feeling. An imageless substance handed through my wife to my shaykh had renamed me Abdul Wadud, servant of the Loving One. I pressed down the side window to catch the slim twilight chorus. Colour-spotted leafage overhead and in front of my windscreen, grew to black shapes, tall windless guardians of my secluded site on the edge of St Albans. That pre-time servant sufferer lingered in my sub-thoughts and his words, 'I worship and adore the true and living God who created all things.' My mixed origins would have to be tempered. Jewish-Christian and Islamic beliefs swelled my transcendent concoction and now the latter, the last, bubbled to the top. I drew up the window, turned on engine and head lamps, started to push back the darkness. I drove to my assigned literature event with less a sense of achievement than I had once savoured. That evening *itfar's* 'idle' has become in my biopic a turning-point, a slender acknowlegement of the founding of a new energy before I rushed off towards the past. I would rush off towards the past many times before at last the idling conquered.

> Behind twilit cloud
> before opening my fast
> Islams of colour: columns
> sacred trees at St Albans
> before reciting poems.

Enroute and Arrival: the east coast

on this long journey
allowed to eat through the hours,
if so, with regret

a Muslim pilgrim
sits near the spirited sea
barely a wave breaks

a *du'a* for home
the western aurora sinks
below horizon

hear in seclusion
the oceanic beat within
die in-to its Lord

in strange servitude
feel that Beloved's seeking gaze
on your downturned face

in a warless heart
touch of the sweet Creator
past imagining

a small scent bottle's
bronze syrup stays unreleased
till sun streamers fade

last hour's human-ness,
as if the world's end deferred
abstinence ripens

a lightning wash-up,
unsipped soup ready to serve:
guests are called to sit

belly aches passing,
best blue our oval table,
we supplicate, praise

buoyed hands in prayer
a bird nest in late summer –
living and the dead

with sun-set's new day
remember the Loving One
never thanked enough.

bismillah hir-rahman nir-rahim

The Artist

to J.M

The artist as a child began his life with mirrors. Not accepting their illusion, he plunged through, smashing the glass, bloodying his hands and arms. He saw reality in the perspective where the room exists beyond its portrait, the coloured walls narrowing toward an invisible point. He not only drove his tricycle into the mirror to arrive at reality, he rejected what stood behind. He was propelled out of the ordinary impression that the mirror reflects us, but prevents entry. He claimed the room rejected him, forcing a flight through the glass to discover his realest home. I wonder if his teddy, a first love object, went with him; shared the cruel awakening carried the speckled blood of a greater rejection.

Your parents cringed in disbelief, longing to throw you, the artist, back into the womb. Plunk out a sane baby, though dreaded the act that might have given you a brother or sister, a living mirror you might have trusted. Their love could not conceal their refutation. Between two massive Nos: the home your parents dominated and the mirror where you crash landed, there prevailed little room for yes. Your toys levitated among dancing lights unsupported by bulbs, shades, angle irons or brackets. Your toys, like possessions appeared to be escaping, needed special negotiation to be brought down to be touched and played with – soon to misbehave and desert again. Yet, you embraced the secret sacred gift that denied immediate affirmation of your desires and affections. Those lights seemed to be illuminators, as much as competitors trying to steal your love-objects. Your parents were around to confuse you further that none of this pain or joy was authentic. It was imagination, subtly perverse and anti-everything they believed. School little help. It had no reason to confirm your miracles, the miraculous, you experienced. It taught you though; gave you tools, weapons perhaps to fight the madness and keep your parents at bay. Instruments could not give you back their love or tolerance.

You guessed without much instruction that art was the answer and could lead to love. You gained strength creating a beautiful thing, as a mirror you entered and explored. The interior that is more than a reflection of the outer, that becomes more than its opposite which allows warping and deviation. You guessed that the heart or where narrowing curves or dark brush strokes led would be elusive and not quickly revealed. Art too carried a profanity that invited entry without arrival, like one of your lights.

The heart remained neither outside in your mis-functioning birth-givers nor inside. Where was it? By early adulthood you were an artiste, gleaning knowledge from college to advance your technical skills and also married, with a young son. Then one day your motorcycle went off the road and your head cracked open. It turned into the scattered fragments that had to be arranged into fine art. You survived. You had changed, reverting to the boy who flew through plate glass. Your wife left with your son. Your career vanished; not the art but the prospect that it could help you provide for those whom you had come to love, or nearly love, approximating the heart. Your widowed mother and drugs rescued you.

The fragments stay, suggesting you could yet create a masterpiece in oils, a film script, a triptych, an altar piece, a Buddhist temple image. You could. But you live at home, with a mother you hate and you think hates you. You hold a creeping paranoia against anyone who might look in your window to see how you are. Drugs enable you to walk into town; go to the post office; listen through your ear phones; keep you on the pavement. They fail to fulfil. Doses leave you longing to re-write the past, to re-ride the motorcycle; come indoors; hug your wife. Your son in her arms or reaching up to you.

Somehow we're friends. I sit across from you in this half-empty library. You are unfolding your portfolio, your art books, your drawings. Do you remember how I once tricked you into saying the *shahada*. You pledged a belief in Allah Almighty? Perhaps the momentary lapse into your supreme gentleness, trusting my intentions, may rescue you in the end. At times I have shown other strange moods, which you noticed; no one has interpreted or comforted except you with your carefulness and insights. Nevertheless, I don't know if I should be sitting across a mere table from you, seeing that every woman in town thinks you're a stalker, seeing you're banned from each restaurant, café and bar, knowing you can tell, in lurid phrasing, a father how beautiful you think his eleven year old daughter is. I realise you can be unpredictable and start flailing arms, growing three times your height; blast my ears with profound wisdom or wildest concept: Doris Leasing is your mother and you were once Omar Khayyam. I do not care if you were that Persian poet and have transformed whom gave you birth. I can't hide my pleasure at your dare. Almost beautiful, if absurd, to hope for impossibles, to be so unguarded.

I have never seen you raise your hand against anyone yet everyone fears you. Never seen you remotely violent. You are different. That's your curse. Oddly I feel in danger sitting across from your swirls of black hair, boxer shoulders and inspector's eyes. You claim you are no longer young. There continues to be the art, your drawings that fascinate but do not appease my apprehension when you intimate that you have more reasons to like than to hate me. Edgingly you argue most enemies can be friends. I have to puzzle what am I. I can not forget the day you told the female staff in the library that every poppy field was an acre of blood, and their reaction. Your art stretches between. I am quiet, not suggesting this face would be better without scribbles across it, or that image would be more inventive if you restrained from forcing it into ugliness, a portrait into a near monstrosity. I accept your need to show that everything everywhere is on the verge of an abyss, an engulfing terror.

Your cross-hatching buries a pretty face. I think I understand your perverse desire to hang a crude veil across beauty as if too much to see what your life could have been in the brassy phizog of what is. You call pictures your cartoons. Sometimes I see a potential, a slip in the negative cant and you produce a startling figure that is held back from your dungeons. It stands delicately, tenderly poised. In an image, in creative rendering on a visual plane, you represent a sorrow as if all humankind could be aware of its Creator, but feels separated and estranged from that Love. Then you illuminate that:

'These are only sketches, the place of real art is elsewhere, a different place. At times I'm there but can't stay, but mostly I'm far from it'.

I know you are recovering ground, keeping your art safe from praise, keeping me from your task. To survive is your motive. You only can persevere by that schooled lie that nothing of value prevails in you, that tale connects past and present, making a destructive whole. To hope to advance your talent is too dangerous. But something else is in that estimating – that you might arrive and breathe in that place long enough to recover the shattered splinters and create an invaluable thing. I imagine the boy-artist who drove through glass to find the reality denied on this side, in time will find love unblocked, companionship restored. He will express a true totality, inner and outer, love and its opposite as One.

J.M. went out of my life some years ago.

May Allah bless, guide and protect him.

Thunder Afternoon
during Ramadan

in honour to my wife who took a
vow of silence as part of her fast.

You won't eat – to rest
and cleanse the stomach – or talk
to soothe, clean your tongue.

You let the phone blare.
You put your hand on your heart
and I turn speechless

like a sounding box
every passing sound vibrates
in your day's silence.

Now, in loud meadow
far beyond the cricket grounds
by a wisping stream:

a queen settles on
her cushioned throne – a bee lands
on purple knapweed

I make quick *wudu*
catching first drops from deluge
in cupped crinkled hands

the cooling storm swirls
like arrows in a vortex
thin sun-blond grasses

fast from onyx ranks –
topaz, ruby, beryl – a half
rainbow gems the east

for your afternoon
swifts, pulsing and screeching,
abstain from our sky

between thunder-shocks
my dripping shifty shadow
is a missing friend.

My heart takes the vow
to listen more. Mallards swim
pleased their path's refreshed.

I pick goose-weed burrs
off my clothes – then lift the latch
to your calm garden.

So much sorrow dis-
appears, without a come back
in our un-telling.

Ramadan Moments

I

a curved
thread of light – in a photo
Medinah's moon

its clinging shadow
the resonating sound-line
of a plucked string

one white flower
this second is like a slumped
double-scoop ice cream

three white-turban sheikhs
bowing towards the ka'ba
iris after rain

hover fly lights on
a tomato plant's curled leaf
en route to the heart

the five o'clock sun
creams almost every leaf
on the burgundy hazel

my dear wife complains
chimney rooks are too noisy.
But what can I do?

I no longer can hear
swifts swifts zinging zinging
through evening's night

on the listed
post office roof
the incorrigible pigeons

I anticipated
so much – didn't notice when
the campanula burst

latest to arrive
soonest to depart,
without feet, leave their mark

around date-shaped clouds
streams of forgiveness –
day flows towards night

The Tender One makes
scattered rings of brightness
pinks, rouge, yellow, blues

a dreamy blackbird
sings and trills as if obsessed
with someone it loves

from a curtain pole
a Syrian green jubba hangs
cut in two by brilliance

through black wings
of ornamental cherry
a facetted moon

our neighbour's lit drive
crunches under his tyres.
We share from a bench.

II

 If the salt pot is tilted
and the high window ajar
who has the patience
to not pull it close and not
spill a grain of crystal?

III

Goddess combs her clouds
leaving a quiff or two
to thrill her admirers.

The brawny Co-Op guard
teases the pretty check-out team
whom tease right back.

If only to absorb
a spoon's ring against a soup bowl
be in the present.

From half an onion
cut patient slices – each one
a yellow-white rainbow.

Poppies give quickly
their petals to the next poppy.
I cling to my frail bloom.

IV

Rain drops start and stop
raspberries again for iftar
a miracle each one.

Forgiveness brings
longing to repent leads to rescue
from night of nights.

adhan to adhan
so many come to listen
who don't breathe the air.

V

Alone with Beloved –
my wife welcomes my crunching
on hot cheese Doritos.

We're ready for flight
on two angled twilight rugs
no void in between

seeking inner peace –
whether or not the warm hours
trigger night thunder.

VI

Is Life all we understand of life
when so much more surrounds us?

Tiny black flies on the white rose are
obeying their duty to the Greater Rose.

An instant you and I feel the Invisible
and cannot pretend it is the nibbling wind.

I announced, I feel under attack, you said,
of course, you're on the path to The Beloved.

Did you give salaams, a greeting of peace, when
you crossed the door-stone to the empty house?

Did you address, bismillahir-rahmaanir-rahiim
when you stepped back out on the empty street?

When the poet is talking foolishness – listen in
peace, you might hear the murmur of the Beloved.

At our time of age we forget more and more – that's
fine it leaves more space for us to remember Allah.

VII

My grandfather wrote, 'we come into this world alone
and alone we leave it' – at last I have no dispute with him.

Shaykh Efendi once sighed and said, 'o people, you can
be right and still be wrong'. Of course, only Love is right.

VIII

Donkey's sick flesh drawn down by a thousand immoralities.
The one who cares for the donkeys will pin them on himself.

Is there a drop, just a sweat-drop of wisdom in such stupidity?
Watch out! When the Beloved touches – donkeys sprout wings.

IX

Is anything impossible for the Beloved?
Can the stars contain the fragrance of jasmine?

X

I'm frightened we have entered the last ten oceans
of Ramadhan – without certainty we can wade across.

XI

Between the white frames of the narrow window – Subhanallah
Between the green berries on the holy tree - Subhanallah
Between the clouds with an lining of blue silk – Subhanallah
Between the terrace rose and raspberry canes – Subhanallah
Between lightning flashes and thunder claps – Subhanallah
Between forgiveness and terror – Subhanallah
Between Allah and his angels – Subhanallah
Between Allah and his prophets – Subhanallah
Between Isa and Muhammad peace be upon them – Subhanallah
Between the beginning and the end – Subhanallah
Between hope and despair – Subhanallah
Between the martyr and the long living – Subhanallah
Between Allah Almighty and the Shaitan – Subhanallah
Between the mountains and the hills – Subhanallah
Between Mekkah and Madinah – Subhanallah
Between love and hate, between truth and lies – Subhanallah
Between day and night, summer and winter – Subhanallah
Between the new born and the life disappearing – Subhanallah
Between spring and autumn, sun and moon – Subhanallah
Between faith and doubt, dream and reality – Subhanallah
Between constant and the always changing - Subhanallah
Between the spinning earth and farthest star – Subhanallah

Between river and ocean, tideline and island – Subhanallah
Between slow notes and rapid, birdsong and storm force 10 –
Subhanallah
Between this world and the next – Subhanallah
Between the coloured threads of a rainbow – Subhanallah
Between the bold looks from a filly and a colt – Subhanallah
Between all that is and all that isn't – Subhanallah
Between the facets in an insect's eye – Subhanallah
Between our heart and mind – Subhanallah
Between toes and our fingers – Subhanallah
Between our legs and our waist – Subhanallah
Between body and soul, between flesh and bone – Subhanallah
Between every heart's pulse and morsel of food – Subhanallah
Between dishes on the table and fruit on the limb – Subhanallah
Between the raw dough and the baked loaf - Subhanallah
Between oasis and the endless desert – Subhanallah
Between ascent and collapse of empires - Subhanallah
Between passion and love, between impure and pure – Subhanallah
Between the petty and the sublime - Subhanallah
Between every salted wave, every spray drop – Subhanallah
Between victory and defeat – Subhanallah
Between male and female, ebb and flow – Subhanallah
Between child and childless, wealthy and in need - Subhanallah
Between the curse and the blessing – Subhanallah
Between remembering and forgetting – Subhanallah
Between Jerusalem and the ka'ba – Subhanallah
Between the ego, free will and destiny – Subhanallah
Between known and unknown – Subhanallah
Between time and space, each bead of a tasbih – Subhanallah
Between each breath, each sound of cymbals - Subhanallah
Between truth and beauty and all ye need know – Subhanallah
Between the dream just dreamt and the dream realised – Subhanallah
Between what we say and what we do – Subhanallah
Between good intentions and bad upshots – Subhanallah
Between anguish of illness and happiness of health – Subhanallah
Between life and death and far and near – Subhanallah
Between Allah and his Angels and the Prophet Muhammad – Subhanallah
Between Allah the Creator and Allah the Destroyer – Subhanallah
Between the hope of paradise and fear of hell – Subhanallah
Between marriage and divorce, separation and union - Subhanallah
Between good and evil, fate and freedom – Subhanallah

Between all that Allah gives and all that Allah takes – Subhanallah
Between the fast of Ramadhan and the feast of Eid – Subhanallah
Between all that Allah raises and all that Allah lowers – Subhanallah
Between standing and prostrating – Subhanallah
Between the rule-conceiver and the rule wrecker – Subhanallah
Between submission and courage, Layla and Majun – Subhanallah
Between 'humility is endless' and 'every angel is terrible' – Subhanallah
Between killing of the innocent and pardoning of the guilty –
Subhanallah
Between the promise and the fulfilled and the unfulfilled – Subhanallah
Between host and the guest, between army and the shepherd –
Subhanallah
Between war and peace, brother and brother, sister and sister –
Subhanallah
Between mother and father, between the lost and the found –
Subhanallah
Between smoke and fire – Subhanallah, air and breath – Subhanallah
Between the traumatised and those that bear the world – Subhanallah
Between the terrorised and the oppressors – Subhanallah
Between victim and victimiser, the vulnerable and too strong –
Subhanallah
Between nightmare at dusk and the nightmare at dawn – Subhanallah
Between the luminous rings of Saturn – Subhanallah
Between the countless branches of the Milky Way – Subhanallah
Between the countless names of Allah – Subhanallah
Between the names of the Prophet Muhammad – Subhanallah
Between the named and unnamed – Subhanallah
Everything that's visible, everything that's invisible belongs to Allah –
Subhanallah, Subhanallah, Subhanallah.
Between the bereaved and the newly buried – Subhanallah
Between our grave and what the Angel speaks – Subhanallah
Between who is your Lord and what do you believe – Subhanallah.
Between the Wabbie and the Sufi – Subhanallah.

XII

Its bronzy-orange face
     a potted lily wavers
          pimpled with raindrops

shakes like a ragged
   flag from a wreckage-marooned
      wounded young sailor

quivers – its six-petalled
   flower-mouth open to accept
      the twists of summer

this garden sailor
   lost in dark knots and snares – now
      seafaring in view.

No green buds to come
   no one cuts your stem – leaves you
      the last wavering.

   XIII

Stars are swimming tonight. Between Night of Power and closing the

sky on Ramadhan – Subhanallah. In the Take-away eating *iftar* the owner

says, he doesn't know if he should be sad or happy at Ramadhan's end. 'A

great test seems to wait till the last few days when the ego is leaping to

taste the freedom of eating when it wants,' my wife at dinner remarks.

These few days have been hardest as if I must be challenged before the

closure to ensure the reality of the fast. Giving up food and drink is the

peel of Ramadhan's fruit compared to its core its pith which encourages a

denial of every nuisance that damages the soul. Stars are more colourful

than my usual power of observation allows me to see. Basil has a scent

like Jasmine for those who chop and prepare in the kitchen.

It comes down to love; our capacity to love, which must grow for the fast to be fruitful. Who knows what has changed one year to the next? The year turns and Ramadhan moves with the seasons and passes through the seasons on the moon's cycle of crescent to full to crescent. The solar year stays at home but Ramadhan migrates through the year and touches each season each character of nature and of human. Each constellation has had and will have its Ramadhan. Every month of fasting embraces at a different phase in the year another mood of love – a spring love, a summer, a winter an autumn love. We must love through every style of duration, a lesson for the human being to accept endless mutability. At the close the moon is left behind; every Ramadhan concludes with the lunar in darkness as if we have stepped beyond image and formation into an unknown of fragmented lights. Some times of the year in these longitudes the fast is so short in hours you forget at noon you shouldn't eat, at others the fast is so long you forget that the middle of the night that you should eat. In the event of love often we distrust a deep loyalty.

It was strange that this year on the last day of Ramadhan, I was going to a funeral. It would have been no less out of context to be invited to a wedding. The self's demise whether through the body's decomposition or through matrimonial union is no goal. The person is seeking something both less and more than either ritual. The death the individual pursues has no fatal illness though it may entail a long struggle or can the mind hope for that destruction through intimate connection with another mortal though such commitment might inspire the heart towards a range of selfless acts and attitudes that predict or prepare the self for dismantling. At Ramadhan's finale the attendant believer might fear little has been achieved. And the moonless glow might cause pain, a dark mirror reflecting failed hopes.

We own no entitlement for this feeling – we can't guess how far we have grown towards our disintegration. The selfish I's death, without that sustained higher love's awareness, appeal and grace, whose existence if conditioned only by our faith we would have long despaired, faltered and hated the thought of abstaining.

Submission to that unconditional presence that love is so much in our practice we hardly can imagine a state of being in which that Most High and Blessed One, The Tenderest and Most Merciful, doesn't exist. Or let us put it this way – that Supreme Being so occupies our intention that we only forego our daily bread to honour His command, not to try to measure with our flimsy faculties the range or velocity of our advance towards matching that selfless love, the One Creator possesses for His Creation. This Presence holds stars and sky. Colourful stars are not dependent on or fixed to the sky, or is the expanse of the universe fixed or clinging to the stars as if it would be lost without their guidance. Both move and appear independent from each other since they are linked through their Creator. He knows also our death-day and marriage when the real Ramadhan is complete.

But so those minor acts or flings of selflessness that have no benefit to us – our physical selves – those deeds nevertheless strangely benefit us more than food and drink, riches and fame. And each Ramadhan we are more conscious (perhaps more than at other times) of these slight exertions into the domain beyond the ego's region, into a peculiar landscape where the renegade love holds out or awaits our attention or stands on tip-toes with a telescope ready to capture us at least for the night. How at odds with world to find ourselves out of bounds sometimes, off planet, a captive of love and stumble on ourselves performing actions and manners which oppose our best mercantile and emotional interest but which sweeten every drink we sip and make sublime the food we eat. Our manoeuvre beyond regulated actions is the mysterious cause for our joy that follows at times the denying of self for some other and ultimately for none other than that unapproachable, unknowable and most Tender Conceiver – Allah.

And I wonder what sequence of events would precipitate an ultimate push that my self would lose its footing and realise such a reversing of heaven's river and a de-starring of the sky whose resulting void is a completeness beyond our knowing – beyond this knowing, at this moment, at the end of this Ramadhan.

XIV

a bloom of blue
announces the dawn-pink
climbing hollyhocks

XV

So precious are those moments when we vanish from our egos that you

Allah our Creator, hide those instances from our gaze, when we escape

from our self's controls when we step into realms where the concentrated

'I' cannot survive, but perishes in a rarefied atmosphere where only the

fragmented 'I', that almost no 'I', can take in that higher than mountains'

air. Subtly you protect those moments. When vanished from the ego

we must be blinded, deafened, made cloddish and a fool otherwise we

would scream our distress and ruin the beauty of our feats. But, you,

more merciful than any can reckon, store up those escapes, our break-

outs. Yes, the tally clerk passes the evidence on to the ship-hands on to

first mate on to the angelic lieutenants until You at the helm, the captain,

reads the chart and sees our selfless moment and records it and scrolls

it up pressing it to your heart – though we may not notice the deed.

And no cruelties, bad thoughts or rows can undo the seconds we slipped

beyond our ego's harbour and entered the seas of altruism if such were

possible. If we were allowed to see that flight or height we might consider

the attempt pathetic, so quickly the ego takes over and lies about our freedom. The challenged 'I' in pride stings us to dismiss our vanishing, calling it incidental, a mischance, dangerous, a toil without worth that earns not a bit of wealth, fame or pleasure or power. We want to forget swiftly desiring to believe that an 'I'-less action is meaningless. But You hold sacred what we would discard.

So there is much hope in our absent-minded-ness, in our not-seeing, not hearing, in our being unable to track down each action of effect to some discernible cause. And in the gap between what we know and do not know – Subhanallah. In the gap a Sufi Shaykh once dreamed he saw the second Khalifah in paradise, Syyidina Omar, and the Shaykh wished to enquire respectfully what actions in the honoured companion's life had admitted him into bliss. The Shaykh reflected on the man's incredible record of victories over the Roman legions, the conquest of Syria, the defeating of the Persian Empire and expanding Islamic rule over many lands. But the second Khalifah said, no, to all these remarkable achievements and explained he had been granted paradise because on one morning he rescued five fledglings that had fallen from their nest, picking them one by one and placing them back into the twig and mud swaddling. Whether the action was fruitful or not was a secondary concern. The Shaykh listened amazed that a humble doing could receive a high station. He bowed in his dream and wept.

XVI

Funeral Rites on the Last Day of Ramadan

It was not my intention to go to a funeral during the last gasp of
Ramadhan. Day 29 of fast brought the usual question from disbelieving
non-Muslims 'surely you're allowed to drink?' I entered the car-park of
the crematorium, the many rows of saplings, at first, didn't make sense.
Inside, I took my place among the simplified wooden pews in a mourning
suit, the light from the hot day through the un-stained windows. The
atmosphere was churchy but the vital signs had been removed. None of
these observations mattered, I was here for the people to share in this
moment of recalling a life and saying farewell to a friend who given time
would've become a great friend to my wife and me. But time wasn't
permitted. She had passed away during Ramadhan, a non-Muslim
honoured with a death during the holy month. That fact set a halo around
her life of kindness. And a week before at our house as we performed
dhikr, a ceremony in which we chant the names of Allah, her presence
entered through the French window from an easterly direction – the
same as that from her home nestled among the Wolds.

When after an extended time I heard the heavy crunch on the approach's
gravel (the crem's doors open to give ventilation) I did not turn round
to see the black limousine drive up. I did not turn round when I heard
that distinctive weighted clunk of the passengers' doors, I knew the

chief mourners, the family of the deceased had arrived. When I heard the pronounced steps of the pall bearers I kept my head forward, then I listened to loud sobs and shutters of the women that followed the petit coffin, the wounded female warrior inside, as much as we are all warriors and deputies of Allah on this planet. Eventually I wept too, my Lord that your precious gift of life you give should be so generously withdrawn like a hand that offers a saint's beard hair and I bow to kiss that hand and then when that hand is removed and the perfumed sacred hair is put away I'm in sorrow. How can it be otherwise but that we celebrate your great gift and grieve to see it vanish behind the closing curtain? Maybe there's a tincture of relief that the sufferer is released from their pain, but this thought will not constrict our tears because we'll remember her in youthful life, vibrant and happy, her each day painted in bright colours. Her husband and son grabbed each other steadying their sobs. Profusion of sunflowers – their big heads drooping – spread over the casket.

The humanist guide from the un-ornate pulpit called up the family members to give their tributes, and symbols were used to show the different facets of her existence: heart shape of roses, two large toy butterflies, images of her garden. The humanist guide nearing the close, touching on the committal, asked that we carry her forward in our memories and recollections in already crowded hearts. There was no appeal to angels, or for a cosmic gust to sweep her into an unearthly tomorrow. And of course you weren't mentioned – not in any of your names. I wondered if it mattered, knowing if you thought a display necessary, you'd show yourself more swiftly than lightning and louder than a thunderclap right overhead. Naturally you stayed quiet and incognito, an observer from the wings. I marvelled again at the Power that's so powerful it doesn't need to use force but waits with infinite patience until we – some of us – call on You. But I know only Your absolute listening allows our calling to be heard. No beatific pinions to waft her off. The guide exerted us to transport her soul towards its destination, as the pall-bearers had brought her body in, now we were requisitioned to carry her out. The humane leader said now the body is coming to its natural end, in the flames.

I guess clicked on fire is as natural as spaded earth but there are many who believe the soul is tortured in those harmless crem flames. I wasn't in any mood to dispute with the organisers and you didn't interject. And all I could do was hug the chief mourner and wish him peace, and the tall man in a colourful tie said, thanks for coming. But I wondered if You, the creator of bodies, required a body to resurrect a body. What do you do when a jet liner smashes into a mountain side and what remains of us are shreds of skin, bits of bones around the black box, are we souls lost, have we out-sped your speed, gone way out past your limits? Then I remembered that You transcend all that we ascribe to You, think of, feel for, believe in or imagine or claim as You. Fire devours, but the soul is not scorched.

I was glad when I read my phone – a message from my wife – come home I miss you which gave me a chance to cool my over-stoked imagination, offer farewells with a final hug and scan across the saddened yet recovering faces and begin to drive across the sun-creamed Wolds back to sensible expectations of our last *iftar*.

Looking back there was a footnote or two, those saplings – some sturdy and already tall others short or needing special plastic tubes to secure their growth. I wandered among them, an immature forest. Someday the crematorium will be hidden from the A road, a woods of remembrance will encircle the burning house. Few were my height, as I walked I read small tilted plaques in substances more perishable than stone. Some stalwart trees trembled younger than other teetering specimens. One inscription among the expectant 'in loving memory' stood out, on a board, a perhaps irritated wife had given her last word 'I told you I was Ill'. Of matter of fact You know the ins and outs, peculiarities of that episodic phrase. You are partisan with us, erasing our misdemeanours, never our little virtues.

XVII

I arrived home exhausted at 4.30pm, five hours approximately to break of fast. I striped off my outer dense clothes, my mourning suit and white shirt and flung into bed for a nap before *asr* prayer two hours ahead.

Slept soundly tickled by dreams but couldn't recollect scenes. Woke up gone seven to my wife saying –you can't sleep anymore, it is *asr*. There was no bucking the orders to get up, make *wudu* and prepare to pray the late afternoon *salat*. Afterwards stacked pots demanded attention from yesterday's dinner and morning's *sahoor*, the meal before the fast which began about 2.30am. The sun was still strong and at about 45 degree angle; the clothes were picked off the line and folded in an oval basket, the clothes pegs in a yellow round one, were carried into the house. Leisurely day was dropping through into night; African swifts left their invisible vapour trails, no expectation of a moon shadow east or west. My spouse and I hugged a few times in passing, not too passionate during hours of abstaining, and no sniffing of flowers or wearing of perfume. The air started to grow cooler, more moist and peaceful. Daylight's traffic din on the street out front had quietened, the pigeons roosted in the deserted building out back, some billing and cooing audible. I answered correspondences; my partner picked raspberries and blueberries for *iftar*. The sun was 20 degrees now, hardly above the roof lines and tree tops, sinking into expectant clouds. It was nearing the time and in the last hour I liked to work on my poems so I shut down the internet and opened my documents. Then I was called in doors, two mobiles phones on the blue table cloth, offered faintly different versions of time. The table was peppered with goodies, my black tea under a cosy, by our two placemats a glass of warmish water and two dates – following the *sunnah* of the Prophet Muhammad, some white slices of coconut, bread in a scooped basket, and soup simmering on the cooker; half a grapefruit for me and cut up pieces of a honey-dew melon for my wife. A small bowl of raspberries and blueberries and Alpine strawberries under covers. I called the *adhan*. She extended a coda in praise to the Prophet. We stood close our feet aligned with the *ka'ba* and with cupped raised hands enacted a *du'a* supplicating for our special concerns. We sat down and began our small meal, water and dates first. The blue-blotched cloth, washed so many times, held delicacies and snacky nibbles; soon we were back on our feet to pray *marghrib*, but not before we shared *eid mubaraks* and our sleeved arms were ravelled in a serious cuddle. When she began to eat her salad she said, our lettuce leaves have been warmed in the sun.

XVIII

Ramadhan's last apricot glow on a listed building's
Red Rasen brick, out back, and apricot lily wavering
from a crock like a soldier's flag stuck in a mound,
leads on to clusters of mid-ripe apricots on the tree
clinging as if an infant to our outside kitchen wall.

Below, a courgette's gold-funnel expands to receive
searching bees; in a day its flower opens then closes.
And we puzzle, from among our desisting days, what
has been fertilised, what hopes will mature into future.

What out-come is more pleasing to the soul than love?
We'll recall how Aisha cared for her husband and would
not scheme to ask who do you desire more, me or Allah.
She loved so, never to test her man's heart, knowing she
existed naked as apricot and courgette before her Creator.

First Day of Ramadan

the new moon didn't
expose her shy curve

a westerly threw in my face
the scent of summer roses

the damask overwhelmed
pebbly slanted tiles

a few streamline *devlins*
careered below stratus

the white clothesline prop
had nowhere to stand

a pre-sun-set bat zig-
zagged high over sky-lights

from its favourite perch
a blackbird's song turned erratic

temperature too low
for mosquitoes to pierce

the garden bench stroked
with rain rapidly dried

the shed moved another
smidgen off its mooring

I distributed blue slug
pellets round lupines

gave two half-ripe
Alpine strawberries

to a local friend who'd
helped me pass the time.

White Night of Ramadan

A hot sun's fortnight
shrinks water to sibilance,
tall grass bends their ears

on time's slipping by
an old man stops to converse
where rainbows once leapt

looping the lane's lamp
shadows of mammoth-winged moths
play against the wall

distant white sheets flash,
gurgles under the culvert,
cheeping of ducklings

two, in mid pond, dance
in blessed randomness round
their mewing mother

a thumb's width above
bats scratch infinity-signs
on the vibrant air

dry foliage soughing
a raindrop pricks my wrist and
leaves a small bubble

between mounting clouds
the full moon of Ramadan
supplants wildest dreams

from upstairs' chanting
you bow down into *sajda*
while I watch outside

closing around night
– serene and total – a Love
no one can offend.

A Ramadan Night

Drops on every sleeve
of the burgundy hazel
holding the sun's stream

rain-seeds on petals
of an in-vase white iris –
you, My Beauty, give.

Water through pebbles –
under the kitchen sink's tap
sahoor dish and spoon

to ceaseless patter
around the lit-up cottage
fragrances turn wild

through dark a drumming
deluge washes the deep pink
off a damask rose.

my sleepless neighbour –
his son nearly killed himself
a few nights ago

unfurled on a shelf
documents of past murders
any soul can read.

Ramadan Journal

dedicated to Shaykh Shamir

Treading on a log
concealed among sweet grasses
it crumbles to dust

white horse chestnut flames
in the rain – 'the birthday tree'
we sometimes called it

a needled rose bush
snatches my green prayer-hat
before in flower

a queen's taffeta
like snowflakes scented petals
drift across the sash

king-size sheets warble
on the line – avian calls
all day imprinted

forget-me-not hearts
countless – another bead on
my burr wood *tasbih*

*

Steve and Me

'I remember you from the arena
café... a writer aren't you?'

among dandelions gone to seed
buttercups close before light's end.

'I gotta sign on tomorrow. I'm
taking the train. £9 on the bus'

I never know if he's going to talk
or walk by – his rouge skin's a veil

'when I get back I'm off celebrating
with four cans of lager ... want join me?'

compion, stitchwort: one nestles
into the green – one rises above

his eyes seek a way out – my brother
I hardly know. Today you've stopped.

'They beat me up down in Dartford
and now they push me down up here'

You created a few nice phrases if I
remember, back in those arena days.

You don't beg booty, wearing both
your shoes 'see you around', you say.

A bee cruises the dark blue and white
hawthorn mottles and scents the trail.

Your eye-slits hunt the light, my friend
of many years, your taut skin's no veil.

A mother brought you into the world
a father once warmed your tiny hands.

*

suddenly
white blossoms
on a dangling hawthorn branch
extend as white blossoms
invisibly into space

Prophet Muhammad (s)
legislates 'sit down, stay close
close to mother earth'

'Lord love a duck' on the far
side, mallards keep increasing:
first two, then three, now four
soporific on the green slope

a moorhen asks me
'I muse how far my ripples
carry – to your heart?'

*

Please don't swear in front of me.
You wouldn't in front of your shaykh.
Pretend I'm your shaykh, then pretend your
wife is, then pretend a leaf is your shaykh.

*

'Jum'a Mubarak'
a friend wears a sherwani
sky powdery blue

*

rain-expectant-clouds
a female blackbird teeters
on the cloths-slumped line

in yellow waistcoat
a blue tit pecks at the end
of the frayed clothes prop

almost full the moon
performs a cameo role
in night's mystic play

*

webs of slow clouds pulse
patches of filigree light
above sparrow chirps

*

Strong growing light dissipates the moon.
A blackbird responds with enigmatic trills
infusing the silence the stars leave behind.

Earlier peace came dropping slow to mirror
W.B. Yeats' phrase, a peace that passes all
understanding echoing biblical lexicon and
from the Jewish faith in wholeness *shalom*.
Peace too is one of the 99 names of Allah.

A Sufi chants at first light, 'You are peace,
from you comes peace, to you returns peace,
let us live in peace'. ..and later in the same
du'a 'Your abode is the abode of peace'.

I know my house but I don't know from
where peace will fall. Earlier between
iftar and *maghreb* peace formed a pool
between break of fast and sunset prayer.
This time Peace arrived upstairs. I was
closing blinds, pulling curtains readying
the house for a still cool nocturne in May.
I stood ready; soon as my knees touched
the prayer mat the peace emerged like an
unseen pattern woven in the rug's design.
I knew at once it was peace, no imposture.

You can do little to earn this munificence
except by being ready to breathe it in, alert
to its potential among other guests to mime
Rumi's poem 'The Guest House'. I know
there are thirteen steps between upstairs
and downstairs, but I can't measure in
which section of home peace will settle
an invisible nest for its patient presence.

I began to pray and peace hovered around
too young for wings. Yet it was more than
vaporous, it reached inside and dispersed
doubts about the cause and need of the fast.

Quietness in my heart and questing in mind,
not since I was abstaining but because Allah
willed the peace. It was in exact time; in this
precise space it could be given without fear.

It's hard to imagine how a human being can
savour being alive unless peace arrives from
time to time, unexpected, often uninvited until
suddenly it occupies an odd corner of the home

and radiates. We wish it never to depart through
door or window, but to stay, stay. Yet it always
departs, has to, without warning or preliminaries
Peace returns to its Creator, Cherisher of worlds.

It returns from where it came to the One to whom
it belongs. Here, you own not a mere loose thread.
The house may be in your name. Peace absconds
with no opening, returns to Source of all belonging –
reminds in absence that you must return the same.

We do our worship completing the daily five *salat*
but none of our acts compels peace to open its arms
to embrace us: the weak, the sick, sleepy, the exiled
the deprived and depraved, to hug or sit beside us to
share in the task of preparing for a new pink-sky day.

Don't let me be proud in belief to whisper to the self
that I am not like those desperate souls. Don't let me
claim I have no need of the Peace-giver's generosity,
because without that Mercy none of us could breathe.

                          *

        The middle-age moon's a bubble.
        How the torn walls of red bricks
        shimmered in yesterday's twilight
        now more red with today's dawn.
        Once more I unfold my prayer rug.

                          *

        buds of masquerade
        look like tops of minarets
        coming into view

        waning moon's shawled in
        satin turbans to honour
        the friends of Allah

*

your first green-pink-touched
strawberries appear – you're not
here to watch them grow

*

Allah exposes us clearer than
an x-ray, reveals for our gaze
the flaws, misdeeds, offences
that slant our living towards
pain, grief, anxiety and want.
We are responsible, have been
given the task of changing our
misfiring nature into a servant's
obedience to the holy ordering
expressed through sacred texts.
Yet those same sources expose
a potential for all of us to repent
and being forgiven via the same
One who spoils our each negative.

*

so little rain still
irises bloom during night
three white sheepish clouds

*

The Mosque Party

after our *iftar*
the mosque carpet strewn with chips
the kids go crazy

they've been hushed for hours
now with snack delights – burst like
fire-crackers with joy

how will some mothers
and fathers soothe, draw them home
perhaps with star-nets

doors slam and elders
come along to pick up flung
Styrofoam cases

a pink hijabed girl,
covered each inch, riots with
prayer-hatted boys

they will never sleep
this side of tomorrow's dawn
till back in the fast

I imagine them
at one with the universe
teasing Muhammad.
sallallahu alayhi wa salaam

From Three Dreams

1.

I'm among entangled railway tracks, twisting across each other, on the surface without a destination. Close behind is a long manufacture building? It appears like the last day of its enterprise whatever was made on the site. Everything's greyscale but not night. There's no activity. I'm wandering around careful not to step into a switch on the rails. I seem alone. No workforce or visitors. The industry's closed down, it could be the steel works in Hamilton, Ontario or in Consort, County Durham. The sky is pillowed with dark smoke. Then a child emerges, not bothered by the environment, walks towards me. She or he (hard to say) is dressed in grey, wearing a hooded coat; it's colder than they're used to. Nine, ten or eleven years old. Stretches up kissing me on the cheek. I accept the gift of affection but fear the police will demand redress or someone will. The vegetation is scrubbed out to a dull matt.

2.
The industrial complex has vanished. I'm in doors, wearing black. The space is crowded with people, in family groups, chatting and circulating, many. I can't see through them to the outer world. I appear to have no involvement. I remain detached. A vast onyx encloses the room that looks to be without windows. Suddenly he or she is there coming into the chaos walking towards me ignoring everyone and everything. From the right. In black garment matching mine. Dusty perhaps. A face bleached against apparel. They walk over. I'm paralysed and can't disappear into the social commotion. Have to stand; they approach. I'm hardly ready for the request; he or she creeps and hugs before I can react, kisses me on the lips, which I wasn't expecting, huggling my face in small hands like a china egg.

3.
I'm outside by a sunny emerald terrain, the industry, the crowded ballroom or conference hall replaced by a beautiful landscaped garden. I'm alone once more. Deciduous trees backdrop this oddly vacant stage on which I stand un-alarmed by the absence of much I once knew. I have

nothing but am included in the space's space. Yet I stand in readiness for a mission. Then, the child appears. I forget my initiative and focus on it. The same child keeps to their harmonious entries strolling with a greater confidence than before. Clothed in threads of silver and gold, a long garment trimmed with jewels at the neckline and around cuffs and hem which flares below the knees. Without a coat, sparkles in their male-female apparel. A profile, radiant and rounded; each limb browned, relaxed. Their bronze hair uncovered shines. He or she reaches on tip-toes; seals my breathing with a kiss. I embrace and awake.

*

frail soft ears of white
in the rain quivering on
their pinnacle stems
the wind's snipped a rose
of yellow which I set in
a flute of water

*

more gossamery iris
further into Arcadia
purple tongues curve
down with gold-speckled
fringes in their grooves

*

converging grey-whites
a swift, so high up, appears
from the next spectrum

*

if you look deeply
among the espalier limbs
you'll see small green plums

*

blue-tits up-side-down
pick off aphids from under
emblem leaves and buds

*

the damask rose bush hugs
an extravagant head
of downturned petals

*

a clothes-pegged black sock
falls into a water jug
that the wise would've moved

*

the morning gorgeous
afternoon brings cloudy rain
and tall stems teeter

*

after *taraweh*'s tranquillity a shaykh and I,
with cups of dense coffee, talk for hours.

To discover a young old companion suffers
in her artistic mind, perturbs night prayers.

I recall, in a room, she looked skinny
as foil enveloped in a leopard-spot wrap.

In a moment she shed it; sneaked away
from the tiny gathering to attend her hurts.

None followed, not her mum, father, sister.
We chanted *zikr* in faith she would return.

*

a bee disappears
into a maze of yellow
on a rose border

*

huge wrinkly dates
in a small porcelain bowl:
the first drink, water

In Bradgate Park

Seeing a fawn through soft bracken
reminded me of my last visit here –
when walking between her parents
a slim girl-child seemed invincible.

in the stream stone-art
that children have constructed
re-routes the murmurs

a female mallard
with her pepper-dots of
ducklings following

preening white plumage
two colossus – their cygnets
between far below

every paddling duck
leaves an expanding
fine rippled V behind
them, across the water
an extended tail of Grace.

*

My *jubba* shifts from
grey to grey-blue in this light
at post-noon's eclipse.

Some frightened to be in the world seek, not knowing what's wrong. Or

why love of a caring mum and dad is not enough to ensure fulfilment.

A young girl near where I live keeps running off. She's nine. When I see

her mother in a car park she says 'not for the first time'. I fear for her

daughter who wills to desert her home. A good home I estimate. Glad she

keeps returning, rubbing her soles on the welcome mat. Wish she would

speak her dancing schoolgirl mind. Share her angst. Perhaps faith would

reach and embrace without touching.

She double braided her long blonde hair. She ran away in the evening.

I picture her under a hood of escape (sneaked off) resting under a river

bridge for a time, where a kind old couple live and leave their gate unlatched. The light, warm evening encouraged her absconding. Her retreat is more than attention seeking this self-eloping and real evading. She watched the water's currents or the ducks skidding down from the clouds, the waving of grasses: this urban girl. When she darted off, it was into nature. Where would she go in our town? Which path elected would lead to an interval of non-civilisation, some other dimension far from the wheel of her hamster exercising in its cage; lately another present – a black and white cat – more parental concessions attempting to hold her to home.

What irritates that she wants to depart from this security? She was once first, then second, third, then forth, in a sequence of births; brothers and sisters could be counted and perceived that way. I was once first then forth in our family's serial. I no longer can feel the trauma that might have spun me about like an empty glass container in a game called spin-the-bottle. But can these shifts in blood relations be so unsettling, that the first born wants to escape? It is close to Ramadan's end. I'm awake in deep night. She'll be asleep, subconsciously preparing for the school day. But school might be the enemy and crass encounters with peers. My friend is beautiful maybe other girls are jealous. She, without the strength to oppose them or ignore, is afflicted. I'm doing a du'a for her in my Ramadan's 29th day of fasting before *iftar*. I know it's easy to slip from being at peace in a loving familiar place to desiring to disappear with speed and leap into the night. Being alone with your own manner of self is one lure of running away. Discovering who this mortal that shadows you is, that leaves an imprint of itself on the day that's past, on the future to come. We yearn to be intimate with that imprinter more than ordinary life can tolerate. Distractions fail. Escape from the group leads to residing with that self, being alone with it. I sought separation from conversant and communal, in the same breath years ago in adolescence, that led by minute degree to degree to a final gasp of Ramadan for this year.

My longing to be alone persists; has become sublimated into fasting, prayer and meditation. Despite the empathic sharing involved and benefits and hopes in that togetherness, I feel remarkably this has been my Ramadan, my running away, more organised than once, still a scuttling into some deeper consciousness of whom I am and my temporality. Tonight when after *zikr* the Prophet's (s) beard hair inside a glass tube was handed round to murids, I took my turn and pressed the phial against my heart. That mysterious organ burned, became active, not functionally, but deliberately affected by the touch of that relic enclosed in transparency. A miniature sleeping beauty, which reaches out and heals with the sensation that in it is preserved some great lover's holiness. Retained and transmitted, handed on to many others: a rare virtue it extends past breathing into another being that conserves and restores. By the sacredness of the one who once held and trimmed those beard hairs, by his beauty and light of intercession I do a du'a for my child escapist friend. She has her destiny. I pray for her to find her specialness which will enable her to belong but also explore that necessity to be detached, seeking a less known vision, to value this life and its complications, to be with her family and yet separated. I know an unique impulse is at work in her longings to elude ordinary expectations which I also seek especially in Ramadan.

She sat, no doubt legs swinging, out there, on an edge of normality in some parti-light in a secret locale, an unknown den, tree house or cluster of trees disguising her. She felt estranged from everyday stresses of home and school. She appeared to search for her cave of revelation. May she find it.

That quest-instinct has arisen. Yet it's hard to imagine, from where on the surface of her sensibility, such adventurism has spouted. She seems entirely a baby-cum-girl child of the materialist modern affluent age, yet desire for the opposite, that disregards danger, has somehow taken root. Discontent is often the sign of a longing to embrace some-thing more nebulous and truthful that can't be supplied by school or the quotient activities and affections of home. She runs away but pursues also, seeks an invisible reality that frightens but sustains. Maybe that longing for a small exodus will find expression in prayer or art in a means to remain within reach and yet approach the unreachable.

An 'unreachable' already looks through her bedroom window when the household is in deep slumber. She responds to its call; far more than fleeing from, she flees toward its absolute sincerity. We can hope that her encounter with that delicate power will be kind and beneficial, not destructive. But we, practitioners of Ramadan feel for her mum and dad too, we absorb their fears that she will fall victim out in this cruel and dangerous world beyond her home's gate. We feel pity for those, who our own desertions leave behind, stunned at our wanting more from earth-time than routine achievements in family and business. Their contentment with the everyday is not to be mocked. We cannot be shamed either because we pursue less servable and profitable goals that we find near impossible to explain to a beloved, a family member or a friend or colleague who wonder why? 'Isn't life hard enough, why make it harder with fasting, prayers, meditations?' Enquired once my kid sister.

We struggle with loved ones for an universal answer. Yet the cosmic pull remains that guides us from commonplace and conventional. Perhaps for me, and a nation of others, the holy month of Ramadan is a signpost of a counter-direction. It presents social harmony and individuality as shared objectives; in the same moment, the month of fasting and greatest mercy, trains the migrant heart towards engagements with the unknown with both group-and-self-shattering revelations. We resist but repeatedly dive into the supernal, emphasising our craving to abscond from the practical and respectful, to pursue and belong to the unbelievable as if turning our human nature into an angelic nature, like being confronted with visions and insights that frighten our everyday sense of whom we are. We accept that such searching is but partially our running feet, slumped heads or our fingers playing the music of the spheres through our *tasbihs*. The unknown calls us to this quest for a higher purer register of existing of feeling, thinking and willing. We need to be connected to that Other's, Divine Other's blessing, guidance and protection. I recognise that my shaykh provides a vital nexus between me and the higher powers of mystical reality. I pray that those powers protect and direct my friend leading her to find earthly guidance from a distinct human being she can trust and honour with faith and love. Are her 'running aways' the first frail urgings of that search? This Ramadan closes. I do not know if I'll be here to see it open next year. If you are, please perform a du'a for my run-away child-friend. She will still require our prayers.

*

A discontent worshipper
arrives and asks for a du'a
I feel my shaykh's insistence
cupping my wrinkled fingers

*

Bonbons for Eid

Transparent boxes inside
with Brother Shamir
among the toffees.

The carnivalesque swirls
around Parrk's sweet shop
each scent clings to us

Owner and patron's
wild banter shows Ramadan
nears its sticky close.

We frisk one called *Nerds,*
through Hollywood colours seek
longed for substitutes

for kids and ad-ults
to swell post-fasting tummies
with treaty darlings.

Hawking at home still
smelling blooms; one more honeyed –
this Sufi chants praise.

*

on the baking sheet
castor sugar silhouettes
from curved Eid biscuits

*

The passion that follows a conclusion can be memorial. I felt this

rhythmic idea at the Ramadan's cessation. Logically Eid follows the

fast, an informed celebration that marks 'after hardship comes ease'.

That excitement with renewed companionship and feasting can reveal

or obscure. I'm talking about a more secretive aftermath, a whispered after-shock, that suggests how the heart might turn towards revelation, greater self-awareness. We're amazed to discover how silent, unrecorded this alternation in our actions; yet we are passionate about change. What follows the celebration has to be more than fading memories of our previous encounters with fate, faith and love. I mourn Ramadan's vanishing and see its later festivities as no equal to that forfeiting. Maybe it is the disproportioning of time and space that compels us towards another perspective. One, if strict, of Eid, fails to balance thirty days of abstaining. The quick eclipsing of Eid's merriment makes me question its meaning. Perhaps, though the mystical has always appeared short against the pragmatic day; the former's outer limitations disclose another means of measuring. Why are we not given thirty days of feasting after three of fasting? Could the human body endure this bias towards lassitude and freedom? And in a sense Ramadan was ordered. Eid is chaotic. Could we survive perpetual anarchy? Yet such unregulated existence might be the highest achievement for the reformed soul to realise, like a father and mother who accept from their loving embrace and conception came the birth of a deranged child, a puerile heart of utter disharmony and disablement: a aberration, a contradiction to natural causes. Somebody, more often shunned then welcomed, a distorted infant who, years beyond their maturity, will require fathering and mothering, an intimate fostering.

We are always on the verge of confessing that we cannot bear our own reality. The creative Greek mind saw the origins of the universe as Order emerging from Chaos. Christian and Islamic holy texts suggest that the disturbance, after a short sharp shock of paradise, is never-ending proposing a need for redemption and salvation. Greek imagine-ers foresaw being saved as extraneous because nothing or everything was lost. Hades prevailed as everyone's destination. Their formula allowed for earthly tragedy; mortal catastrophe was part of the universal symmetry. No redemption survived in Death's kingdom. All that could be heroic stood on Gaia. This concept is put into the mouth of the dead Achilles when visited in the underworld by the wandering Odyessus. The great warrior exclaims, 'By god, I'd rather be a slave on earth for another man … than rule down here over all the breathless dead.' [Homer's *The Odyssey*, Book II, 556-8, trans. R. Fagles] With this orientation, Greek imagination privileged training and knowledge; portraying apathy, anger, lust, greed, envy or aridness of spirit or pride (causes of misfortune) as absence of knowledge; not as defects or sins, contingent or innate. We, from monotheistic traditions, feel there is something more than intellect to be rescued and something surpassing knowledge to be lost. The ancient paradigm didn't concede to the potential of humanity's free-will that could be mystically remunerated or penalised. John Milton in his epic *Paradise Lost* through the voice of Satan presents the human paradox, 'For only in destroying I find ease/ to my relentless thoughts … ' [Book IX, lines 129-130] We know this is a false 'ease' but acknowledge and believe that God, Allah Almighty, orders the universe but has nevertheless permitted the invasion of human freedom (with its sometimes demonic intent) which often disrupts His plans until He as supreme authority reasserts His will to contain the choas humans are allowed to create against spiritual judgements and living bionetworks. We marvel Allah allows us to destroy, towards Armageddon, his pristine and beautiful Creation, as we anguish Evil had a passport to enter Paradise.

How long could we endure Eid's indulges before we fainted in an ogrey of exhaustion? After how many days, would we long to return to Ramadan? Strange, that we elect 'hardship' over 'ease' but certainly the sane do. Allah allows us to give birth to wreckages which are the consequences of our own doing. Yet we stand more amazed, how sudden and total His intervention can be to redress the balance and go forward to forgive and put his mercy so far above his anger, showering his blessings on the earth-bound. Allah can forgive with such transcendent mercy that it shatters our reasoning of what is ethical as if a brick was thrown through a stained glass mosaic. He forgives whom we would damn and condemns whom we would pardon. Our understanding, the scope of our laws and moral manners cannot intuit this other-cosmos of divine wisdom and love. Confronted by this absurdity that defies our proportions we become atheists or embrace Allah's light-filled abyss, His extremist endgame. Definitely we have to give up notions of how to measure what is proportional, in balance, a golden mean, also the prospect of rationalising the reality of God. We have to release our ingrained perspective for another point of view that, though, transcendent and superior, will sanction our weak and temporal attitudes and moods to conquer and cause inevitable damage. If we cannot believe in totality we are called on possibly to suspend our disbelief. In a sense Ramadan is Allah's gift of 'return to order'. With Eid we have a chance to serve the One who demands no service, we have a moment to give to whom doesn't require gifts, to love as He loves; forgives, whom doesn't need forgiveness or affection.

The birth of innocent disorder, like a child everyone despairs of, is the thundercloud of our mis-actions and sorrows, shot through with lightning of Allah's grace. His grace extends the opportunity to embrace what, with our acquired knowledge or orthodox understanding and logic, prevails as indefensible to embrace. Except we find love in our hearts to endure the Creator's truth that can be revealed as distorted; in need of vast repair. His love can seem a warped mirror-image to the passing on-looker. His beauty can be shown in the jerking speechless gestures of a juvenile whose expected maturity and educated independence is never to emerge, who needs nurturing until the end of his life.

*

Yellow by yellow
wild iris, water lilies
along the Witham

My Mum Passed in Ramadan 1438 in Canada

dedicated to my family

The Soul Traveller

I wondered if I might
meet you up here
over the Atlantic, mum

the view, the propulsion thrills
and the inserted seat screen reveals
fissures in deep ocean contours

experts say our love-bond
is oceanic. I have never known
how to interpret that

I have travelled across the jet-stream
often enough – your 'good to see you'
this time will lack sense and breath

the ocean below looks unfathomed,
is that what they mean
our affection must be deep?

Then how could I vanish
decades back only to re-appear again
and again like a migratory?

The Atlantic's wide,
we evidence the gulf,
our nesting cliffs abut far apart.

So why am I speeding
over a cerulean ribbed surface
home to your last ritual?

You were a traveller
of six continents then confined
to two rooms and a corridor.

Your last morning,
I'm told, you gazed at the ceiling
and acknowledged no one.

I have faced your love gaze
sometime – shall we be bonded
 at last in absence?

Years back I claimed
I wanted to be a poet
you shocked with 'you'll suffer'.

The atmosphere radiant,
clouds linger like white confetti
in your bridal hair.

Someone will hold you soon
dye your curls, perking you up
for your funeral-appearance.

With advanced ageing
we grow wise, skinnier and skinnier
until we disappear.

 Someone will weigh sacred pins
lighter than a tern's feathers –
how much greater must that love be?

I never fantasised this high flight.
That's dumb. Of course I have.
It's each woman's and man's fortune

we human beings share
dual destinies – the act of birth
and the instance of death.

You once offered me birth –
I snatched it. In a demented way
I'm handing you death.

To my Mum Ramadan, Canada

In the plangent aftermath
of night-long thundering
the leaves of your ancient
Maple tree discourse

from the foliage drips, drops
on the wooden back porch
that your other son constructed
its sliding door pulled back

through its screen I hear
the first creatures create
their rare provenance
their unique calls, their trills

hardly a smidgen of light
and they begin to record
and announce. My head's
in *sajda* on my prayer quill.

And you passed away
a week ago in your 100th year
at your visitation in your oak
coffin, you rested, made-up

a scarlet sliver for lips
your eyes sealed, your
skin still bruised but icy
in a yellow suit jacket

that your daughter chose
shiny pins of significance
fastened to yellow lapels
a black blouse beneath.

I bowed down and kissed
your ringed, locked fingers
the veiny back of them
and tasted your absence

I sat at a distance
and observed and watched
as I never could have
when you had breath

and could yearn for visitors
and whisper of trees as final friends.
To my bleared sight you became
between each tribute's fragrance

stilled into landscape
a profile of an unexplored
terrain where this being dead
is marked as illusory as life.

It's Ramadan. I have
prayed through cloud clashes,
lightening's rips and chocking rain
the night air sneaking in

and you have stood beside
me, your fingers clawing
and clinging as if you begged
to be lifted from torment

I was frightened and
speechless, paused
before my next plunge
to the angled mat's zero.

Were you in hell
mother, pleading for me
through faith to release you –
had the angel condemned?

Then you were luminous
alongside my panting
you breathed new oxygen
within a vibrant interim

between death and parting
for a time could illuminate
your beloveds, to ease them
in their grieving for you.

The bird-songs increase
with each added drop of light
whirligigs of whip-poor-wills
sweet repeats of cardinals.

As salaam alaykum, mother
I honour my birth-giver
to my startling you respond
'wa alaykum salaam' then add

'don't be shocked that I
appear from hell one moment
and paradise the next – I'm no longer
under your world's understanding.'

I didn't guess that you would
know the language of salaam.
'All languages I can disperse
since eternity is in my voice.'

I crunch my head
deeper into my prayer mat –
the month of the fast and hope
the devils are enchained

and love is easier to inhale
between first light and sun-rise
and coolness searches
through the screen door.

My mother retorts
'you speak of love, look
into the surrounding void
see it singing with love

remember when you all night
perched on a heather moor
and watched the full moon
brighten and arch across space

how the moon, to natural eyes
still bright, dulled, became hollow
and how the nebulous space
grew radiant until tactile

the object had become
without substance
and the vast emptiness
had become substance.

Remember when you
read the Psalms years ago
recall how at instance
not of your contriving –

at an instance the Psalms
started to decipher you –
the inanimate book was alive
and you the lifeless pages

turning. Don't shun reversal.
Yearn for it. If you come to
my grave with a pure heart
I will rise up to meet you

if you come with a black
and a mind full of the world
you'll see and feel only
stiff words stylishly cut.

Think how you came to
your Blessed Shaykh's grave
how he came out of his tomb
for a long second and greeted you

did you not see the green
agnate ring on his finger
aglow signifying a life
searching for reality?

I must part now
but this parting is
no parting – a million
more will pursue

and still no parting.
Listen to the dawn's
chorus – each frail
note belongs to the One.

Listen, sink deeper into
your prayer's bruised fabric
until there is no way left
except to turn to God.'

In Home's Summer Garden

i'm my mum
Lorraine Sutherland (1917-2017)

A shadow moves
like a chipmunk
over her rockery

I listen for ...
a female cardinal
lights on her fence top

under the June sun
flowers of solomon's seal
dangle in hiding

a cloudless expanse
shadows riot on ours
and next doors' back wall

a perfume expands
across restored grass-patches
dwarf chinese lilac

three backyards off
children squeal and holler round
an imagined pool

peony's ball-buds
remain closed, I won't be here
when they flaunt their pinks

a dad starts shouting
'Hot Dogs, Hot Dogs, Who wants them?'
The kids go silent

a statue fountain
– a gift from mum's husband –
stays open mouthed

usual suspects
two squirrels chasing around
the maple's stone bark

a gull's white wings
high up give a pattern
to infinity

film noir shadows
creep towards our back decking
cooling my wonder

three rock-steps descend
on the tilt, a branch throws down
an emblem of bark

day's sweetest songsters
grow subdued, over the way
the children never ...

on and on shadows
stretch out toward the promise
of light's tomorrow

lilac scent deepens
bringing melancholia
to my griever's heart

quick scooping whistles
her cardinal approaches
through twilight's growth.

Twentieth Nocturne

Mid-way through clipped night
I pull close a rose and find
a red ancient book
if its thick leaves are cut through
it will squeal with secrets.

In black and then blue
in life still entering death
through the moon's last quarter
those final ten fasts – we read
all our missing passions.

I am amazed why time
transforms the view of how
we see what once passed before,
why, against our scheming, some
desires are transcribed as love.

Three *fajrs* in Central London, UK

Among frond and leaf
at Sufi murid's mansion
a shy robin cheeps.

Host and guests discuss
number four's subtleties
under art nouveau lamps.

On the tasselled lawn
the three days we've felt 'at home'
a kid's ball hasn't budged.

Across untimed views
he unravels giant shutters
for Ramadan's night ...

alifs of moonlight
across *fajr's* prayer rug –
a foot behind him.

My wife and I visited, one Summer an extraordinary artist, spiritual thinker and conversationalist. He creates large calligraphic paintings of *arabic* in vivid colour combinations. His art shows letter-shapes as abstract patterns. If their meaning can be read or not, is less important than the viewer responding to shapes, colours and proportions. His work is famous: an exhibition in the Vatican and commissions from royalty. Our discussions moved across many topics – underlined with the relationship between contemporary and ancient traditions. He refers to archetypes seeking Eternal Principles that embrace opposites, promoting the faith of Islam and Oneness. A polymath, he illustrates to us how the hexagon is fundamental in building forms and determining magnitude. He speak about geometry; the significance of Arab scholars in preserving and translating Greek text such as Pythagoras' whom Islamic masters called 'the man of wisdom'. We break our fast round a beautiful table from Italy with him and his son's young family who'd arrived from Africa. We woke early to share *sahoor*; the Dr. preparing a celebrated middle eastern dish called 'fool'. He is an excellent host. I fear we are less helpful than we could be setting out crockery and cutlery. From early morning until late at night, overhead, air traffic whines to and from London airports. Yet serenity pervades the vast roomed house: its walls decorated with the master's art and Qur'anic calligraphy. We dwell on mystic poets; their search for the Beloved. I quote Mevlana, Jelal al-Din Rumi that ethics are vital for an aspirant walking a spiritual path. He cites Omar Khayyam, astronomer, quatrain poet and mathematician, saying he stood 'on a shore we can't even imagine.' I picture Ramadan's cosmic waves shinning round the poor poet's feet.

Ramadan Quatrains
written during *Itiqaf*

(last ten days in seclusion)

1.

Ramadan is not remotely an entrance and exit.
It becomes a wading in, deeper and deeper,
until there's no floor remaining, until you are
a companion of Muhammad on an inner Hajj.

2.

I wilt like a young green without rain
then my head lifts again by Allah's Mercy.
I blanket the windows to not hear motorcycles
roaring to the coast. I seek another ocean.

3.

It looks to be snowing across sand currents
and the palm trees around an oasis shiver
groomed in whiteness. To my imagination
Canada and Arabia glow in a love-embrace.

4.

Such a pleasure to leave behind for once
the islands of disgrace and islands of virtue.
The bow heaves on. I quiver through *salawat*.
World, round or flat: will I fall off or return to self?

5.

Wisdom in the Cheshire Cat's reply to Alice
'It doesn't matter which road you take...'
There's no route less trodden either, only destiny.
Saint Ra'bia says each day we come closer to Allah.

6.

I compute praises on the Prophet and on Allah.
No number finalises this mystical treasure house.
A more miraculous entrance is required. Only with
sincerity can you hope to open Aladdin's cave.

7.

I grieve the victims who haven't had a chance to die
before they died. Death confronted them like a wall
of ice erupting in an earthquake. Would more have
died, before they died, had Death been kinder?

8.

Allah, You are the well that guides us to the well
the oasis in the wilderness guiding us to the oasis.
You are the nourisher who feeds us on the way and
when we reach our destination you offer a full cup.

9.

Muhammad, I saw you bending over a well's edge
thought you were drawing water to quell your thirst.
But instead you were preparing 'to pour the light and
beauty of your intercession' into this ruined heart.

10.

I marvel at the One who created me, though I am
not, at the Divine Presence that shaped me, though
I am not, at the breath blown into me, though I am not.
I hope these 'nots' add up to something more than me.

11.

I received a letter saying 'I had wrongly claimed.'
I wanted to be called grandad when a surrogate.
The letter of course was correct. Only you exist
Allah. To claim I exist at all is to wrongly claim.

12.

Muhammad's father died soon after Muhammad
was conceived, his mother soon after giving birth.
When Prophet he called a stranger his son and stated
not by blood-bonds only by faith is status obtained.

13.

Try not to anticipate the reward of the cloak
no matter how devotedly you pray or perform *zikr*
pretend over and over there must be no such coat
until you have suppressed all knowledge of it.

14.

My Shaykh said 'keep your enemy in your heart'.
I didn't ask what to do when she's no longer a foe.
I picture my Shaykh's response 'fold up your heart
like a fruit stand on the highway – time to go home'.

15.

Inner isles shrink to nothing if we step far enough.
Take a leap beyond into the Vastness, turn and see
already vanished the city and shoreline. One step into
the Unknown is more than most mortals can endure.

16.

Fifth day, in as deep as far as the way out might be,
the hope of fulfilment is alive. Some work's been done.
Hard to assess its value except – a small grant from Allah
that if I fall to sleep, my *tasbih* doesn't fall to the floor.

17.

This inner condition is like you find in the film Solaris.
I have entered a living miasma of irrational knowledge
that throws exact images, moulded by emotions. I cling
to *salawat* to guide me through this supraconsciousness.

18.

This is not my first *itiqaf*, the initial one was easier.
The immediate is bizarrely demanding. I engage each
sensation's colour. The first seclusion four years ago
I have added four more mountains to carry since then.

19.

Not on horizon, if there is an horizon or in foreground –
a form with twin walking sticks crosses middle space.
My surface mind recognises and gives a name and fate.
But what is more real 'knowing' or the moving icon?

20.

Beneath the internal dome of a star-freckled night
light speckles waveless water and the nearby beach
where Salvador Dali's empty fishing boat's moored.
The *azan* for *fajr* pouring through pain-free galaxies.

21.

Sincerity's perhaps the distress we are just able to bear.
I listen to a hammering in the distance and the sound
transforms to nails into innocent hands. The crucified
are in my vista along with Muhammad's sweat, sweat.

22.

An ornate wrought iron fence enclosing an orange grove,
across a willow-pattern plate, a lattice divide zigzagging:
I don't know to climb it or to wait and see who's coming.
I'm worried, I might, unmeaning, offend a mythology.

23.

Here's no birth of tragedy, if you must fight an inner
Minotaur you will never deceive an outward Ariadne.
Here, children leave doors open everywhere and it is
possible to imagine the child Nietzsche dreamed of.

24.

1,2,3 and 4 days passed in a mist then I leapt to the 6th
today. Who or what can be content between 5 and 7?
I weep for the vulnerability of 6. We perform 6 rakats
for maghreb's *awwabin*, 2 threes is a fifth of Ramadan.

25.

I won't ask Allah Almighty to make life easy.
His supreme servant, Rumi, says, 'in this world
to achieve anything you must work hard, in the
spiritual world, you have to work twice as hard.'

26.

Nevertheless 6 became the day the balloons under
my eyeballs burst and rain howled down my cheeks.
My wife avers my eyes look clearer. I'm grateful for
a minor sign that says the Eternal counts all grieving.

27.

Don't attempt to renovate the house that Allah has built.
If a window stares grimly half-open, if recklessly a door
hangs from a hinge or a tile's missing from the front path
these imperfections are nothing less than Allah's perfection.

28.

I told my Ego we're going into solitude and darkness.
Spruced up for the town, I heard him cringe 'I'll kill him'.
Now here we are among illuminations in unseen places
how do you feel? He groans, 'You're still alive, aren't ya?'

29.

Muhammad waited in a cave, not the same as waiting
for a train on schedule or a black cab delayed in the rain.
For truth and compassion and light, un-vehicular goals
with little evidence of eventual arrival, he still waited.

30.

In the upper left, at the full, a moon-burst, as if the River
Euphrates, light flows out to a 'darkling plain'. Muhammad
sits on the lead camel of a *Caravan of Dreams*, then he turns
his head, searching. (Excuse me, I must keep up with him).

31.

A small child weeps stars down her scored cheeks,
turquoise pupils become black ponds in a white skull
that joins the shore's ocean-rounded outliers where
we, after seven voyages, have become observers.

32.

We worship with many *salawat* and titles of Allah
following the train of our beads, not guessing what
might intercept our path. The forgotten's remembered.
Suddenly in our face, final events far away disarm us.

33.

No one with belief should be over-anxious when they
close down their eyelids and this inward terrain opens.
Enter, as if you walked among your ancestors' graves
show homage to unheard-of names as to the familiar.

34.

There could be no roses in the rose avenues today
yet an aged gardener with gloved fingers snips and
hands down to an old mother a bouquet for their table.
Never know who you'll greet in love's soft corridors.

35.

Wasted, after the Night of Power, we can hardly stand.
Doing a hundred *rakats*, before dawn, creates a sanctum.
In that place, for those you have closed your heart against,
in that peace, no logic dictates, your heart must stay closed.

36.

Dismissed by the 'child of no time' hurts, disowned
by the mother of that innocent increases the sorrow.
If they could grasp what God allows, they'd know
a secret Wendy-house exists of peace and sharing.

37.

This door's an anti-door, ebony or stained for centuries,
tresses of lengthy chains hang across its panelled face,
no sign of entry or exit, no keyhole or barred window,
across its lintel scribbled writing - unreadable for now.

38.

It seems this vacuity resembles an inner-caravanserai.
From routes like the four winds my family has gathered
enjoying the ambience. Strangers play music in a corner.
Let the ney-flutes and the *salawat*-wine keep flowing.

39.

You are unlikely to foreshadow who will give notice.
Hushed *Allahs* lead to 30 years ago: vial of May poesy
poetic note, to vast embarrassment, to hostile feelings.
I say 'sorry' and offer a du'a for the slighted human.

40.

In this *itiqaf* it feels I am reclining in my grave soil.
Atoms of my badness and atoms of goodness flash
past, before end-time, for an intimate-eye to examine.
Could force the earth apart, but instead keep gazing.

41.

Allah is the river that circulates to its source with-
out once altering its flow. '...From You comes peace.
To You returns peace, make us live in peace, my Lord.'
Allah's the summit and the veil that eclipses the summit.

42.

I wish I comprehended the way to address this visage –
browned with age, a white beard, a look so disciplined.
Across its forehead there's a line of Arabic calligraphy
as if on a rebel's bandana, instead written on the skin.

43.

The passion for nothing is our recurring theme.
Does at last a bell blare when the bout is over?
'Allah, lift from us trials that only You can lift'
I serve a plea, knowing all this can't be mine.

44.

As in Las Meninas, except in the distant doorframe
the watchful figure is absent. Still, a worldly family
occupies centre stage but as a final remedy for the in-
completeness of being, an invisible painter looks on.

45.

An ablution bowl of mirrors filled with limpid water.
One angle not enough, infinite reflections are needed.
My inner-space awash with blue from one blue stone
– a gift to a child who cried when she misplaced it.

46.

Have I reformed since the eighth day, yesterday?
My right shoulder aches more and my left eye
needs re-threading into place. Follow the *tasbih*
visualise each bead's divide – daylight to daylight.

47.

I wouldn't be nine again, breaking into grandad's
tall cabinet: pornographic and Auschwitz images
sandwiched. Was that the day a razor blade slit
my eye? Who owns the yarn to close the fissure?

48.

Ancient affections may yet be restored. Periplus.
From last shore sightings we tack away towards
Ocean where the fractured visions of Sinbad or
Odysseus are reconciled, neither inmates of hell.

49.

It is as if 'effort' and 'permission' faced in debate.
Is it conceivable to really exert with a poor result
or expend minimum energy with a good outcome?
The ideal: when what we will the Infinite Other wills.

50.

To identify with violets on Bashō's worn road north
dainty petals and stems trembling in westward gusts:
Sufi masters say, draw what's distant unbearably near.
When this empathy's attained, how far off can be love?

51.

As years pass and blessed Ramadans come and go
days have not turned into nights or nights to days.
But it's no issue to see why we pray in darkness' glow
for something great, beyond fate, challenging hate.

52.

Oneness is our sacred undertaking, not conflict.
Fasting of gurus, abstaining of rabbis, of the Zen
teachers, the priest's Lent, the shaykh's Ramadan
play towards *fana*, totality, on another scale, love.

53.

Inner silence erupts in flares of uncontrolled orange
until quietened by red's ameliorating of physical pain,
yellow streams in, all at once submissive blues, then
green, the Prophet's hue, dovetails undisclosed skies.

54.

The sublime child will deny it befriended invisibles
and saw a v-flight of geese like a horizontal mountain
as we ignore our bond with the Creator, until a crisis
shocks us to begin our effort to remember the One.

55.

No lucid link, on a tall tree's bare limbs a bird moves
its neck dark-ringed, with turquoise plumes its thrush
-size form stays hushed. Is this the bird Muhammad saw
with a small beak that held the failings of the world?

56.

There's a single sail on the horizon or a singular
person sailing on a camel's back across the desert
with the Pleiades above his right shoulder. Now he
swallows sour grapes not to disdain an old man's gift.

57.

Our shelter of arcane space settles into obscurity
as if no one could find the route to this sacred void.
Now, the softest white gold floats across the dark's
serenity like Yusuf's coat or Muhammad's mantle.

58.

Only goodwill and forgiveness can breathe
in the fathoms beyond the contriving mind,
no rage at a neighbour may or poison thought.
You love destiny and love your destiny denied.

59.

We cannot remain earth-favoured, we must depart
to nothing, or into nature or a part of us continues.
We feed the body, can we learn to feed the soul?
Our inwardness taps on the threshold of the guest.

60.

Sometimes the shadow of it is greater than the thing
or absence of it can be more pronounced than love.
The end's the beginning, beginning can be the end.
Sometimes the ocean spreads far without horizons.

61.

In this moment, the slope of the meadow hints
at a more potent beauty than summer flowers.
We forget how close Death is to our sightline.
The inmost rain and wind helps us understand.

62.

This supreme perfume is like a fire on the skin
a present from a Shaykh at the point of departure.
After arrival, reluctant to let it touch, but keeping
what glows in the bottle does not lead to realisation.

63.

It is hard to be true to what you cannot see
to an inner dimension that promises so much.
We know what the heart sees is true, but first
may have to accept for a long time we are blind.

64.

In marriage of minds – what are the greatest fruits?
Fidelity and love and respect seem beyond inquiry.
Out in the ailing world such virtues are distinguished.
Inside blessed here, we may taste the gaps in between.

65.

The real journey begins by negating the journey:
sign posts disappear as soon as we curve inwards.
'End of the world' is a euphemism for this turning
and what we find there is so much harder to share.

66.

The destiny of affections is so frequently defeat –
hurt feelings and separations preclude our hopes.
Outward life cowers from this sensibility. Only
in love's unseen cavity can the heart bear to know.

67.

This aching seems our one gift back to the Creator.
After illusions, this pain can grow beyond sorrow.
With this grief we may enter the cruellest pit and
as we descend more and more blossoms bloom.

68.

Outer notes may grow off the scale as you crawl
inwards beyond superficial reason's watch-dogs,
tumbling of a leaf could reverberate like thunder
a small child's footfalls create another causeway.

69.

Maybe just frantic to conceive one more quatrain.
Where does love go if there's no one to receive it?
Hopefully it doesn't stumble back into the old self
but expands outward till touching the toes of God.

70.

Each seclusion's mineshaft has tumbled in
still I wish to dig. The sky-sun is brightest
inside us, deeper than time and no one comes
to it, but by grace or chance, yet come, come.

71.

Saw him in achy steps on the main street
his back hunched, past the disused banks.
I meet him in *salawats*' inner corridor, he's
held a second, in flight, to receive a blessing.

Towards Islamic Cloud

Mediterranean –
sail-stretched galleons and then we're
almost lost in beard hair

perspiration winks
on the left engine's casing,
skin wrinkles below:

altering seamless
stratus fields buttoned with blue –
I only guess form:

like bowed worshippers
packed in the Süleymaniye,
near continent clouds

through pale sleepfulness
the jet's turbine vibrations
tickle my crossed feet

a porthole eye weeps –
some utter Absence out there
conquers our roaring.

I dream the Founder
had in mind our aspiring
to create this flight

a sweet, mad Lover
produces form – swirls turn back
move to triple-loops:

under unphased light
as if an earthling's unchained –
soul wings pulsating

a starry sky hides
humdrum facts; we plunge, touchdown,
free to forget all.

In Egypt

dedicated to those who serve

Here in Mansouria, mid-way up the Nile Delta between Cairo and
Alexandria Afifa and me are living in a tropical paradise during Ramadan.

You and I hear the *adzan* for prayers and the Qur'an recited at intervals
through the night from local mosques. The sun shines radiantly in the day
and the moon at night. Hoopoe birds tap with their curved beaks into
the grass and clover like a ground cover. Their paradise crests flashing
up and down; they're sensitive and soon take flight. Sparrows are here
and invariable crows and many others yet unidentified. The hoopoes
suggest we have arrived in an ancient Islamic world surrounded by huge
and varied palms and cactuses. Flame trees and date palms rise high
above the lawn and the rectangular bathing pool which glows tiled in
multicoloured greens.

We went swimming or paddling yesterday afternoon. The water is
constantly flowing over the edge of the pool into a trough and re-cycled.
This creates the artistic perspective that the pool has no borders and
flows out in the garden; the leaves and flame petals keep falling, the
bougainvillaea stretches up the sides of the palace with the building's
sharp arched windows and orange-rust-pink painted walls. Everywhere

are signs of a colonial past, ornate furniture, screen in gazebos and fish ponds. I like hearing the creaking/squeaking of long bamboo shoots and the hoopoes *hoopoes hoopoes* like a turtledove in the UK or a mourning dove in Canada decorate the garden in sounds. As you says they must use vast amounts of water to keep this garden green in the middle of a desert. The heat tells us everyday we are in a desert and takes our strength away. But the delicious food prepared for us in the early morning and evening at what they call 'breakfast' restores us.

The palace contains such a range of furniture, ornate chairs by the entrance wall, bureaus and dressing tables with mirrors and a giant oval table in the dining room. The room's walls are embellished with arabic calligraphy and suddenly a vast ceramic bowl or platter dancing with infinite geometric designs, huge as a table, hung on the wall, takes our breath away. Much is in a slight state of disrepair as if keeping this dream interior together is a task beyond human capacity, but the servants and the owner try. Our official host arrives soon. I'm typing in his office now. The room from the floor to ceiling a succession of shelves full of books, his own remarkable calligraphy and books about Egypt and Islam and between the books pictures of Shaykh Nazim. Also framed photographs of the old Cairo, the old Mecca, the days of the British Empire. Everywhere drawings of a more ancient world startle my senses. And piles of prayer rugs in the corners and book-stands and a green and purple turban sits on a waist high table the exact size for the hat. The room's panelled in what looks like walnut and now I breathe in the hint of that wood's perfume whilst out the screened window groundsmen stroll pass and within hearing the repeats of an unknown bird. The fauna is here, last night an enormous beetle scurried across then climbed up on the shelves to have a scan of all this collection of human wisdom. I prayed *isha* in here among literary terraces of genius and love of life.

The old screens fail to keep out the insects. The mosquitoes have borrowed my blood leaving big red blotches on my arms, hands and feet. Perhaps a hundred bites. Each night I pray in the private mosque – another artistic delight with elegantly carved entrances, framework and divides, delicate hand-blown glass lamps hang on metal rings from the ceiling with red cushioned settees, low to the floor, on each side, the alcove can be lit up showing its subtly wrought design in white ceramic. Also the hum of the mosquitoes. Exhausted from prayers I fall asleep then they devour me. With the approach of first light I hear the distant recitals of the Qur'an with earliest birdsong. I'm experiencing Ramadan as I have never imagined. In the mosque exists the most state-of-the-art air conditioning, sending a refined breeze across forehead and bare feet? Afterwards lavender oil soothes my nocturnal sores.

We have servants to look after our washing, preparing food, driving us wherever we wish. We are privileged beings. May Allah grant all of us his Love.

Notes from the Belovéd

Within big shadows
of banana leaves – a fly
caresses both ears

under lily pads
vanishing into darkness
a botchy koi carp

two white butterflies
around white bougainvillea
till the wind divides

brightest, luminous
greens of high high palms shimmer
in complete blueness

skin of the flame tree
looks scorched by its radiant
red flowers above

in the mid-distance
resembling bobbing rabbit
this solo hoopoe

through the afternoon
the soft-noted and shrieker
in turn take the stage

calling on Allah
among trills, cheepings and stops
a small perched Mufti

whose sandaled footsteps
impress heaven – paradise
persons walking by

they deny nothing
yearning yearning what they have
whom none can abuse

a stone curlew
after pattern shouts
settles by the water
then stalking on it stilts
drops in shade again

tracing my skin
a dung fly feels the landscape's
unstable – zooms off

above, a hoopoe –
long shadows toward *maghrib*
a waving red rose

a frail dove's drinking –
sun-spots shrink on a pink wall
by a swaying rose.

Another Day's Fascinations

Specks on wing tips – each
as if a Catherine wheel
paired hoopoes take flight

a green windfall date
ker-plucks
in the pond

day's long shadows,
light scales to the Eucalypts' top,
stretch toward their end

in a mystic stream
along the pool's unseen edge
the flame tree's petals

in its mirror-depths
descend all forms of palm fronds
gathering above

complexity
whoos, oo, oo, whoos, oo oo wee
in the acacia

a highway of bees
glows from the lily-pad pond
to the hive and back

a bulbul perhaps
blackstart, a yellow-tail wagstaff
prepares to *cher-ble*

algae-encircled
a shapely fountain's at peace
where the lizard slinks

In Alexandría

A thousand, thousands zing and swoop
on the wing, swifts, swifts above the city
over the narrow balcony hung streets.
Night coils into day before sun ignites.

Mid-morning and through unveiled
honking, women and girls in hijabs
evening promises in their oval faces
leap in and out of small transports.

It's Ramadan, mid-way through fast.
Leaning against the heated sea-wall
a bald-headed man picks the Qur'an
from his blue shopping bag and reads.

You can feel the excitement in his eyes.
After an age, as if saying that's enough
he stows away those golden lethal pages.
He's ready to hail-down the next microbus.

Stench of fish-smells merge with debris.
Vast solar-waves pound the harbour arms
that, as if twins, curve toward the horizon
as though to a point between two oceans.

Tomorrow, tomorrow, after swifts swarm,
when not one sound remains in the hot sky
he might return, between stops, and order
his eyesight to plunge into the next *surah*.

*

Abu Abbas Al Mursi

I descending, from a mosque, into his tomb-room
after paying money to an attendant, and giving
an advised amount to many petitioning, down a

tunnel walled in green, through a filigreed gate,
under the low ceiling, sweetness in the still air,
preparing to do a du'a by the renewed calligraphy
that drapes the grave of the shaykh, suddenly …

'Don't worry, I'm here'
exclaims the saint
from his old *maqam*
giving a good yank
on my grey coat tail.

The Tropical Garden

Mosquito bites might have made me feverish. I dreamed that this

paradise was reality. Our plummet from grace a bad dream and soon very

soon we would awake to the truth.

With Suleiman's crest a hoopoe *hoopoes hoopoes* laughing into flight

a dizzy flower from the flame tree settles on papyrus

Sat at a table, the bathing pool light pours through the table's wooden

filigree design to decorate the grass and my trouser legs. Five hoopoes,

you, my wife, count, they search into the green with curved bills. Then

move on seeking a new place to prospect for gold perhaps as the sun

pummels and we find shade under big pods dangling below deciduous

leaves. When we swim or relax in the pool no one's allowed to enter the

garden. The surface flows like a shiny table toward the pool's edge and

falls into a surrounding trough which leads on to the water being treated and revegetated. In a self-refreshing cycle, there appears no end to the water reflecting the multi-toned green tiles. It looks to stretch into the garden as if nothing constrains its motion. Sparrows collect along its imaginary fringe to drink lifting their beaks with each sip. A big pink red towel has been placed on a stone pedestal for yours pleasure. The pool is a green flame sending fires of day into shadows that aged trees create.

Remember my love we have never left paradise. Nothing needs to wait for our return. We have not departed. Like Coleridge's Kubla Khan dream we remain to listen, to see, to feel with heart.

squeaking bamboo beside the koi carp pond tantalises my ears
followed by humming mosquitoes waiting for sleep to bring forgetfulness.
climbing in notched steps a palm hangs gold chandeliers of ripening dates
a lover's finger grips a fan – a lapwing lights on copernicia

In the house, the villa, each exquisite item of furniture tells a story in the curve of a tall mirror shaped like an entrance to a temple or mosque. A face is welcoming in the mother of pearl inlay, in the lion motifs on top of table's legs. Heavy doors divide the rooms. A large marble floor entry and gallery which leads up a few steps to the south and north. Across from the main entrance through the broad screened in the hallway, sandaled feet quickly find the exit to the tiled patio and garden. Outside must be always coming into the palace though the worn steel netting doesn't always keep out the insects, the mosquitoes. You say much is imitation and wonder what is real. Our presence is real. The natural growth we observe outdoors transfers its designs along corridors or inside panelled rooms. We imagine who walked or was wheeled here before us, who mastered cultured sips from the china, who gazed on ceramic masterpieces, a bowl, a jug, a child's bathing-pool-size platter on the wall, who knew their narratives, who accepted the love.

Through lattice shutters each facet of glass turns to a waving green cube

secretive drawers and faintly wrapped cupboards can't be left unexplored

I cherish how your finger shows me, in a painting, a moon gives balance

a mango juice jug before permitting a sip we embrace its form

framed penmanship – letters hugging words depth – words rise to letters.

We know they rise higher, ascend to numbers, to values towards infinity.

I leave the doors open, room to room, along the corridor, relaxing chair to chair, to see the half-arches through the house. Before lamps are switched on colours and shadows alternate. One to one, they connect, modern to ancient genius, pictures along the walls, one to one. Though our inactivity may perturb some, it all makes sense to us who live here somehow.

From the screened-in gazebo, a pavilion or patio, we hear frogs punctuate

the evening peace. At a low metal table, more like a huge tray, three of

us share wedges of cerise watermelon, nuts and dried cranberries, dates

and a baked pumpkin dish with nuts implanted over its buff gold crust.

And apricots dried and fresh. In slim glasses our visitor and you and I sip

mint tea with a tempered spoon of sugar. The tea's bronze glow welcomes

the abrupt departure of day and the sudden acceptance of night. Though

the building is five decades old I feel our trio has vanished into centuries

to reappear surrounded with these wickerwork chairs and thick white

tablecloth with an odd flying ant crawling across, smaller than expected.

Perhaps that sudden devouring of the sun leaving a pink ochre smear

hints of violent death. Keep in mind my love we dwell in paradise and

death has no authority here. The table like a lipped shield is inscribed

with a circular pattern – geometric and floral motifs chase each other in

a secret pursuit. Our young visitor tells us about the history of the place.

The founder and first helpers, the privileged earliest residents, cries

of children, mothers and fathers. When the first course is finished he

requests a fresh plate and you and I look on in awe.

The pale green fretting looks like a harvest of grapes by the whirling fans

the interior exudes the scent of unravelling wickerwork furniture

and pillows that have been aired in the sun.

a door half-opens through to another quarter beyond the pink wall

Eucalyptus roots have lifted some of the tiles on the flickering floor

in the purple hour a child visitor arrives speaking of loved ones

some unguarded holes in the majli's screen – existence pours through

I'm eager to wish the dawn's arrival to keep my dream of innocence alive
in which we live forever yet love existence. We know the whispering of
destruction and guilt but we close our ears to its lies. Do you not feel
younger, my love? You look younger and more enchanting, the light
on your face resembles the dawn. We sense the nearness of the desert,
sometimes the wind's loaded with sand. In the garden water arrives and
refreshes the vegetation; the king palm soars to pleasurable stars. After
our early prayers we sleep through the morning. In the afternoon we walk
through the garden.

each creamy flower a vortex of fragrance – this frangipani

Heaven's soft River through green – white jasmine excites my breathing

In the mosque or Zawiyya, like up-side-down goblets lamps are suspended from the ceiling on metal rings, nine lamps each slightly chipped or grazed or cracked, then five lamps with different kinds of bulbs, then one central light bulb, perhaps like an inversed flame of incandescence if we look closely. They linger above the indigo blue wall to wall carpet with vermillion, low to the ground, settees on the east and west sides. Or are the lamps bells that ring with silence that now and then flimmer in a paradisiac wind. The air will move. The air must move. Some light fixtures are translucent, some yellow-tinted, some almost green. The windows of the Zawiyya are stained in ruby ovals with small glittering ochres in a figure-eight borders. There would be a place to worship in paradise, a site sensitive to the creator behind the appearances of wonder which are also from the creator. I love to see you curled on a red cushion reciting *surahs* that no-one has written or can out-interpret their un-inscribable origins. The creator honours no distinction between its own will and what It creates. Such is its love. Each wave of birds is part of that sublimity, beyond gender, creed or any other partition. W B Yeats once asked, 'how can we know the dancer from the dance'. Have we reached that vanishing point, in a lengthening room of bliss, my love where what we love and what we are is simultaneous? Let us be humble we've been allowed to read the words of God without grasping the language. The alcove, a niche to the infinite, the *mihrab* stands hooded in white ceramic designs.

Placid dogs welcome with barks our coming and going but we are always here. The one white the other black each has sniffed and touched us when unawares we gazed on the miracle of being here. Probably a mistake, a time-hole in destiny like a sun-hole in evening clouds, allows us this harmony.

Bare foot an old visitor strolls in the early morning garden, before the heat of the day quietens Attar's birds and darkens thought. Night moisture oozes through his toes. He's put on ceremonial clothes, a green conical prayer hat wrapped around with a fine white scarf leaving a modest tail extending. He's in long grey spacious trousers and a long grey jacket with buttons, again loose fitting. Only the cloth around his turban is tight. He gestures with humility and patience towards the phenomena of being. He dosen't guess how but love's in the atmosphere, the sun shows golden whiskers through the varied leaves still from the night. Suddenly he's aware that an Angel walks with him. Its invisibility and strange-ness fail to alarm. He hears no footsteps or soft padding beside him, no commotion of mighty wings, no laser-burning of all seeing eyes. The Great One's height, width or depth or strength doesn't make him cringe and despair. By the presence of its love the scented trees and bushes smell sweeter. He refuses to call the sublime he or she. He asks what existence would be like without retribution. You're in paradise nothing has fallen out of love, comes a blissful reply. There is no sweat drop on the old visitor's skin; each blemish is washed away. Coolness weaves through the different levels like dispersing birds. Can we live without dying? Again the angelic being gives an answer. He walks on examining, listening for each nuance of the premature day, leaves drip and sun-shadows hardly form; the light's an ochre ball between smooth barked and the coarse enveloped boughs. Does all this belong to Allah? Yes, all this, this, every minute or vast display is His. And also what you do not see yet, hear or feel yet is already His and when you forget everything and fall in slumber He remembers everything and does not sleep. I'm ready to welcome you each fresh morning until you are responsive enough to share in caring for the garden. A forth question is on his lips, but he stays silent recalling the tradition of three. The aged friend is honoured to breathe, to walk by One who knows whom is first and last. How can my life have importance, would have been the old man's query. He satisfies his heart: how can my life fail to be vital if I stroll with a being who knows the Creator, a Presence that steps and plants no divide between dream and reality?

startling designs across nocturnal prayers a stone curlew shrieks.

Final Day Light

Its fallen flowers
like butterflies on the lawn
bougainvillea

if nothing else will –
flies will always desire
your companionship

on a marathon
small black ants follow the grains
on a wood table

fine palm fronds quiver
like fingers that beckoned me
but went unanswered

such a profound gulp
reverberates from so small
an immature date

two caravan chairs
are in long conversation
unable to speak

veils of my eyes drop
what's exposed at some point loves
a moment to dose

we leave tomorrow
hardly knowing the place that has
punctured our skin

around the garden
you drift in a long blue gown's
white hijab and gaze

at ground level stir –
notched banana leaves address
where you sauntered pass

guessing our going
they haven't visited today
those partner hoopoes

arriving with haste
the Egyptian retriever's
one lick says goodbye

quickly the sun drops
from the day's heat as quickly
the night air arrives

in an infant breeze
the palms' grey-green fountainheads
swish beyond their fruit

Qur'an reciters –
voices, verse over verse, rise
as day light crumbles.

Mysteries of Faith

On the opening white night of Ramadan
I came out hoping to gaze at the Milky Way.
But it started to pour. What would it mean if
I could make a drop a star, a pool the moon?

*

Whatever we gain from the depths of our
hearts, we must test in the spotlight of day,
whatever attained from the day's brightness
must be examined in our shadowy hearts.

*

Love is the skeleton key to each doorway.
But the door may not be opened in yours
or your beloved's time. It may only open
when all other keys have rusted away.

*

Imagine the Holy Prophet Muhammad (saws)
with no pages, in a cave, no objects of faith.
Qur'an more than a book: some *surahs* start
with a tap of sounds as if there are no words.

*

At times we act feebly us human creatures.
Then, we pray and address the All Powerful.
But That One makes us wake up and celebrate
in time both our weaknesses and strengths.

*

Allah's great gift seems our freedom of will.
Is it so sacred The Almight must allow our
self-destruction or has The Subtle One another
gift up His deepest sleeves – Infinite Mercy?

Seclusion at Home

in the living room
thick blue curtains drawn across
make a silent cove

dedicated to the lover who out-
lives the agony of rejection.

In three sunny squares
of the north-aligned window
mauve campanula

past my view through glass
mum and child – I know there's two
though I see one

a meander
in a gold river
the handle
on the coal scuttle

as if I could still hold
my old mum's hand
a 200 bead *tasbih*
its thin cordage

campanula veins
intending to build a bridge
between there and here

now a bee rides this
flower-cornucopia
tapping on the glass

my best friend's glass vase
colours from so far away
turns window to door

passing through, seeking
but with so much left
that can't be displaced

with a glowing top
a small bottle of Black Musk
awaits 'end of fast'

wonderful water
my heart's well fills
fingers strain
dividing the beads

child I can't forget
what will I say to you when
you can't remember?

as graceful as
a Chagall nude
the pitted grains
of driftwood

in grey so much light
for intrepid eyes that grip
all the swaying green

Papa
when you crossed the bar
I was 5000 miles
across an ocean

with strident textures
an empty bowl
of laterite

iftar aromas
wafting through the curtained room
disrupt confinement

even-ing's greyscale
reaches the campanula
blue-purples succumb.

Precession

glittering
birds in a torrent are born
from a sly-eye moon

gromwell
lapis lazuli stars
out of green gloaming

a zing zinging swift
so many inter-loop
voice of the cosmos

like the zodiac
the apricot holds twelve
promises of fruit

ancient as black
in an iris stem
Tyrian purple

tangent of snow
under last month's daffodils
alyssum

one tincture to the next
on our quavering axis
the great year flies back.

The Fast

The outer wooden door's closed
and inner shades pulled down
to deflect the afternoon sun, yet
the heat eats through the walls.

No orchard fruit can be nibbled
from covered bowls, or well water
scooped up from earthen jugs
until the sun falls below the hills.

It is Ramadan, the month of Allah's
greatest forgiving, and of our fasting.
Muslim men and women keep
their gaze and curb their tongues.

In Medina, Muhammad's (saws)
young wife, Aisha, has collapsed
from the stale air's feverish fire
and he supports her in his arms;

he says, here my Humayra, my
little beauty, suck on my tongue
draw its deep moisture through
your lips to cool your body.

Imagine this honey tongue has
savoured Adam's bitter fruit,
and declared the redeeming laws
that Musa brought from Sinai

imagine it at peace in the mouth
of Dawud when he faced Goliath,
hear it pronounce words of healing
the Son of Mary gave the nations.

Come, my innocent one, and drink
from my skin – a line of liquid love
let it percolate down through your limbs
and keep The All-Forbearing's fast.

On The Verge of Fasting

From a day of rain
the path be-petalled –
wood pigeons preening.

A darkling blackbird
perhaps its ultimate
song of the year.

The Milky Way –
in between scattered stars
Heaven's meandering.

Courtyard pebbles shine
in countless variations
bound to Ramadan.

Peterborough lyrics

Dedicated to Sufi Nadim. I stayed with him in Ramadan a decade ago.
He described the intense, beautiful, loving and ultimately sorrowful
relationship between his Shaykh, Quibla Alem (*rahamatuulah*h)and
himself as a murid or follower of that Sufi master. A commentator
has portrayed Mevlana Jala al-Din Rumi's Masnevi as revealing the
relationship, above all, between Rumi and Shams of Tribriz. I was
fortunate over my visit to experience some of the mystery and demands
between a Shaykh and a dedicated murid, also to be trained in my Islamic
spiritual practices. Sufi Nadim was given power and presence from his
Great Shaykh who passed away in 1999. Many call on this youngish man
to be given help through his prayers or Du'as. This branch of Nasqibandi
(Islamic Sufi order) wear delicate prayer hats they call 'crowns' because
the Holy Prophet (s.a.w.) said to Qbila Alem in a vision on one occasion –
your followers shall wear white crowns. My Shayhk Muhammad Nazim
L'Haqqani and Qliba Alem often met to share *zikr*, food and prayer in
London.

Traffic's hush sweetens...
after breaking my fast
with white-crown brothers

him and I relax on facing
settees – does he feel like me both
our Shaykhs in the room?

I listen to his teaching
stories – through distant tongues
he makes my heart burn

perhaps when rising
in night's hinterland – my first thought
will be – Allah

from my Nokia's
screen saver my Shaykh smiles
as never before

a 3 am door-rap
the woman across the street brings *sahoor*
under a red-chequered scarf

'These roti are costly',
he says. I ask, 'Why?' 'She wants me
to get rid of the second wife'.

Peterborough black backs
cawing – awake the river
leading to ocean

long white shirt
and waistcoat over pyjamas:
I chant the short *Khatm*

he says, 'on the assembly line
I'm quiet during Ramadan
no food … no talk'

as if past routine
the neighbour's promised food
arrives precisely at *iftar*

his Great Shaykh's *jubba*
stays deep in his closet to stem
others' jealousies

he says, 'the only feeling
to serve is love for Allah
His Prophet and your Shaykh.'

pink blue floral scarves
on white knees, four of us kneel
in four-leaf clover shape

we're out and about, rain pounds...
'the Sufi masters' he says
keep eyes on their feet'.

right, left, in and out,
heart rounding pools, Allah Hu
Allah Hu, right, left

he teaches me the way
to learn, not *surahs* by rote:
but through the heart's *zikr*

he speaks of the sandal brooch
brightly pinned to his waistcoat
that fluttered off one yesterday

him and I face to face
at the dawn's *mefhal* prayer –
two leaves on a branch

him on a twelve hour shift
I wash up plastic cups and plates
sudsing his sourer

gulls high circling
under grey vapours destined to
become thunderclaps

yellow, red, green and black
like inner stations – a scarf
floats from the settee

in a cave five years
Grandshaykh prayed – not stuffing a draught
to keep out the snow

my trainer recounts
'either the lion's on you, or you
learn to ride the lion.'

after tea, biscuits,
he drills with quick sharp Allahs
'watch my lips' he says.

a blissful fragrance
from a Sufi's sweaty gear –
assaults my nose

I let my turban's white tail
slide down in front, imitating
my Shaykh bowed in *zikr*

the sun's desperate
to break in this morning
to abduct my sleep

he admits, he's grieving
for his Shaykh, Qliba Alem
who passed 10 years ago

'I know', he excites,
'just how almost all the *sahaba* felt
when Muhammad died'

the prefect man who
still had a breath that could be stopped
who can understand that?

black-eye bean curry
last night – after the shortest
call from his neighbour

if 'keeping your eyes'
is more than Qu'ran and Hidith,
imagine what those eyes see!

there's a new bird singing…
Allah Hu, Allah Hu, Allah Hu,
and it's perched in my chest

we trade snake-fables,
fanciful and real, one curled
in a tomb, one hissing in prayer

frightened on this path
if I take another step –
an avalanche behind!

a boy on the street
with a drum – someone's started
my heart a second time

turning sacred pages
he doesn't read, until the words
give heat to his thumb

'Wake up. Don't be bored.
And yet don't measure your actions,
but your wakefulness

he quotes the Urdu poet
who wrote, 'The clouds don't look
on whom they rain.'

'I'm coming. Drown me
or not, You are the boat'. The same
voice lands us at the ka'ba

for two hours and more
we rank the consequences of
'to be or not to be'

high up squawking gulls
recall ocean – the vastness
outside each scene's frame

he reveals how to set
my tan shoes on the floor
so I enter the right first

the round kitchen clock
is zikring. 'I only teach …
what I know' he says

if one child begs
a hug he kisses all his children
on their brown foreheads

'narrow mindedness
is a disease' he remarks,
sudsing up dirty dishes

I pray in his room
may my inner-eye spin towards
the Unseen Beloved

opening the fast
he opens my black wrinkled dates
digging out each stone

a Sufi's someone
who's always remembering God
through flagless *zikr*

a guest in a strange place
stumbles over what's a piece of cake
for the homeowner

'My Great Shaykh', he starts,
'had more than power, light came
from love's pain behind his gaze'.

'A man, thousands
of miles off, buried six feet down,
still directs my will'

'My master … left … no chance
for goodbye … stepping from a plane
at an airport, he was gone.'

Sufi Nadim softly bears
my mispronounced *arabic*
knowing it was once his

folding his white crown
he puts it in his chest pocket
'off to work again'

in his long absence
I do heart's *zikr* – hoping
to earn a pleasing word

'Will you give me my treasures?'
I ask. 'What do you think I'm doing
each time I look at you?' he asks.

His Great Shaykh's *jubba*
rests in the wardrobe, I can't help
but stroke its black stitched cuff.

'When my mouth's fasting'
he says, 'the way I see it,
so are my hair and nails'

our tea bags brewing
in glass mugs – we brew ourselves
on tales from far masters

the sky's a plaited grey
the becalmed day I'm leaving
my young teacher's house

when I woke my first
thought was Allah – who pulls apart
the sky, opens the heart

on my bedside table
I kiss the little lamp that's
lit up the words I've read

his du'a gave a baby
to the childless, now her young sister
brings food to his door

'only once' he says 'did
the Great Shaykh's eyes and mine meet
a love-force I couldn't bear'

when the troubled vortex
remembers Allah Almighty
it becomes a timeless space

I pack my suitcase …
he's given no scarf, ring or token
but something I can't name

'of the world: a Sufi's
a bird flying over the sea,
catching without wet wings'

his grieving falters
in knowledge of his Great Shaykh's
unsleeping presence

'I sometimes put on
his coat, just to keep my sadness
contained, held in its sleeves.'

the day comes when the lover
will see his Beloved before him,
their eyes meeting in bliss

'in a week you've learned
what it took me twenty years',
my teacher praises

the heart's *zikr* runs
down my arms and legs, rises
in the head, Allah Hu

a blue velt space,
a white fringe, the whirring gulls
have gone to ocean

dear self, Abdul Wadud
forgive my silence. My lips
tingle with remembrance.

secret on secret door through door,
heart after heart, body to soul, Hu
Hu Hu ...

The Pen

Long palm leaves appear speechless
but listen to the finesse of the reed-pen

in a sixteenth century tombroom's alcove
and right to left across the wall's page.

A master artist coaxes the inked nib
for curves and coils tilting its edge

scraping with a forest rustle, as in *zikr*
when murids pant the names of Allah.

He works fast. The pen swallow-dives,
in flourishes skims. His wisdom tested.

A border contains his scripted universe
he weaves in mistakes for the Sublime.

Each galaxy tells a secret; in-between
abysses gleam. Again his arm in labour.

He grips the trimmed reed to give birth
on stonework, without limning an image.

He calls absorbed viewers to see beyond
form – to compassion, forgiveness, awe.

Notes

Zikr: meditative chanting, 'remembrance of God',
repeating the names of Allah

murids: followers of a Shaykh, adherents to the Sufi way.

Miniatures
from Recent Fasts

*

through protected
foliage – sky-glows
imitate galaxies

*

the cosmic sculptor
gives pleasure to marble –
marble reciprocates

*

gutting an ancient fish –
splitting a butternut beam
with axe and mallet

*

the sun drops below
the *masjid*'s dome – clouds march by
like war-shocked recruits

*

beneath and above
the climaxes of yellow
Allah's greying sky

*

on a chimney pot
before diving to a grave
two rooks chuntering

*

nothing is shattered,
glass wall, in introspection,
slowly vanishes

*

like a golden goose
the last fare in this seat laid
a chocolate egg

*

a speckled fluff-ball
on the green wheelie bin's lid
intoning robin

*

hours hum past outside
a player clicks praying beads –
comets come and go

*

where the moon pierces
despite an ocean haar
through briefest peepholes

*

'these baby blue eyes
cannot close on those who loathe
our wading ashore'

*

a tiger's flood roar ...
last winter's bridge of peace
savaged by monsoon

*

when fasting who can
inhale from the sparse table
tumbled white jasmine?

*

to the oak chair's back
a quivering leaf clings
miraculously

*

heart ache
that stumbles in once a year
this time arrives in Ramadan.

*

joined by Month of Fast
in countless reflectances
every checkstone speaks

*

A friend says, in passing,
this work of poems and stories
and meditations
should be called
a *Book of Feelings*

Last Minute Rush

In the King St. take-a-way, in a windowless room
we plunge to *sajda* on fresh waves of cardboard

he puts me right, once more, that young blackshirted
worker, born into the faith, who calls me brother.

Saturday midnight, last punters hug their fast food.
At times we forget everything and still are blessed.

He knows the Qu'ran, inside out, and among a hot
sink's sudsy wash-up, starts to recite its Opening.

I slip-slide through the door, not losing my balance
on mopped floors, while he envelops the day's takings.

1.30am, he smokes and speaks the language of Paradise
before gazing out his windscreen, flies towards home.

I meander, unguarded, between streams of clubbers
the most radiant moon sends down the sweetest rain.

Eve of Eid

Another Holy Night

Between cloud-fluxes
cut from their tranquil moorings
a few stars at sea.

From the motorway
spray rising – a second shock –
mourning beams wade through.

I feel bereaved say-
ing farewell to Ramadan
for another age.

As Jalluddin Rumi often concluded his poems
'these are only words.'

bismillah hir-rahman nir-rahim

IT

the need for food for water
is suspended

It cannot be achieved
without straining effort
no effort can achieve It

an ancient understood
who said, 'the way is empty
use cannot drain It.'

I used to be afraid
of the phrase
'All things perish
except Allah's Face'

when we arrive my love
you and I disappear
we are It.

if you went to the farthest beginning
It fades to infinity
if you struggle to the last of the last
It slips away to the never-ending
in between like on a string
It suspends a trillion universes

I was doing *salawat*
in praise of the Prophet (pbuh)
when my fingers refused to move
from one *tasbih* bead to the next,
the space between each drop
could not be crossed
like forms of lead my hands sunk
below the surface of me

To obey disturbs It
To disobey disturbs.

Best words in the wisest order
may lead
the sweetest rhythms –
neither word nor music can be It.

Neither living nor dying
not breathing and no ceasing of breath

my heart is a dream
orbiting like a comet
in a vast ellipsoid through space.
When will it return? My heart has not left.

Coming and going disturb It.

To remember or predict
disturbs.

My lips turn to sand
my body crumbles
a wind chases its grains.

To not exist …

The ring of reason breaks for It.
The well of feelings overflows
the will succumbs

If you look into
the clearest body
and fail to see your reflection
this might be near

the beauty of
an elegant woman or man
is a shadow of It
love between mother and child

father – child
an umbra
to seek truth a shade of It

It has no shade or shadow

light, dark disturbs

Tongues go silent for It
ears melt away
beauty and truth disappear into It.

Blissful to disappear into It.

To not exist is the way to It.